PURR
THERAPY

WHAT TIMMY AND MARINA TAUGHT ME
ABOUT LOVE, LIFE, AND LOSS

Kathy McCoy, PhD

Health Communications, Inc.
Deerfield Beach, Florida

www.hcibooks.com

Note: To protect patients' privacy, names and identifying circumstances of those whose stories are featured in this book have been changed, and some are composites. There is one exception: At the request of her family, Mariana's real first name and life circumstances have been included.

Library of Congress Cataloging-in-Publication Data
is available through the Library of Congress

© 2014 Kathy McCoy

ISBN-13: 978-0-7573-1803-0
ISBN-10: 0-7573-1803-7
e-Pub: 978-0-7573-1804-7 ˌ
e-Pub: 978-0-7573-1803-0

Publisher: Health Communications, Inc.
          3201 S.W. 15th Street
          Deerfield Beach, FL 33442–8190

Cover design by Larissa Hise Henoch
Interior design and formatting by Lawna Patterson Oldfield

To my husband, Bob Stover,
for saying yes to adopting
the two therapy cats we found by surprise
and who loved them and all the cats before or
since at least as much as I have
and
To Dr. Tracy McFarland,
the Cat Doctor of Santa Clarita, California,
who rescued and gave us the
incredible gift of Timmy and Gus
and who took such wonderful care of our cats
Freddie, Timmy, Gus, Maggie, and Marina

Timmy

- Marina

CONTENTS

PREFACE

Timmy and Marina:
The Therapy Cats

Timmy and Marina never knew each other.

But they were both rescue animals, both coming into my life when I wasn't looking for a cat.

And they both unexpectedly demonstrated traits that cats don't often have—most notably, an affinity for family, friends, *and* strangers.

Many of us enjoy the loving companionship of a pet cat, an animal sensitive to our feelings, whose love is unconditional and whose sweet, furry presence is so comforting.

But being a therapy animal—especially in psychotherapy—is quite different.

Cats aren't frequently used in animal-assisted psychotherapy. This type of therapy cat, after all, needs to be friendly with strangers, willing to be touched, petted, and held by a variety of people unfamiliar to it. Therapy cats have to be tolerant of loud voices and angry shouting, emotional distress, and sudden movements. It's a tall order for any creature, but it is a particular challenge for a cat.

Timmy and Marina, who worked with me in my private practice at different times, were two very special cats who had unique talents.

Timmy, a Burmese/red tabby mix, was especially good with depressed or anxious patients, sometimes even drying a weeping client's tears with his soft paws or furry cheek. Marina, a flame-point Siamese, would throw herself into the heat of conflict in family therapy—comforting and distracting the combatants until their voices lowered and their moods softened and compromise was possible.

Knowing, loving, and working with both of these therapy cats was an incredible pleasure. Timmy and Marina brought comfort to my patients and joy to my home.

They had something else in common: they both died tragically, quite early in life, like angels lent for just a limited time. And yet, in their sweet, short lives, they made such a difference.

This is their story—and mine as I worked with, lived with, and loved these two very special cats, learning lessons in life, loss, and love along the way.

One:

I WASN'T LOOKING FOR A CAT

The two tiny kittens caught my eye the minute I walked into the office of Dr. Tracy McFarland, the Cat Doctor of Santa Clarita, California.

I tried to ignore them.

This was to be a quick errand, an after-work pickup of another bag of saline solution for our dying seventeen-year-old cat, Freddie. Although he was suffering from both cancer and kidney failure, the daily saline infusions kept him active and feeling good enough to visit with his friends—both human and feline—throughout the neighborhood.

We used to joke that Freddie had more friends than we did, from the moment we brought him home as a five-week-old shelter kitten to these last months of his life. He was still socializing, still very much himself. Neighbor children carried him around and admonished him to stay out of the street. Neighbors who didn't know our names knew his.

Yet this was no sweet, cuddly kitty. Freddie was a huge, tough male cat. He was an experienced street fighter who, after years of battles with neighborhood cats, had established himself as the community alpha cat. He had many feline friends and followers. But they all knew he was boss. Even when we would discipline him for a rare transgression with a quick spritz from a plant mister, Freddie made it clear that to behave our way or not was his decision. Locking eyes with Bob, he would advance toward him, even as repeated spritzing soaked his lush black and white fur. Then he would stop short, turn, and walk away, dripping but having made his point.

Perhaps Freddie's combination of toughness and deep affection for those he chose to love won over our longtime next-door neighbors, Pete and Carol, who were confirmed cat-haters.

When they had first moved in, Bob and I went over to say hello as they stood in their driveway. They greeted us brusquely and added that we needed to know that they hated cats and that they were avid gardeners. They would appreciate it if we would keep our damn cat out of their garden. Bob and I looked at each other with alarm. Freddie spent most days outside. How could we keep him out of one yard? We tried keeping him inside the days I worked at home. But most often, he was roaming free. We braced for the complaints. They never came.

Six months later, Carol asked me to bring in their mail during the week that she and Pete were visiting her youngest daughter in Florida for the Christmas holidays. "Just put the mail on our kitchen table," she said.

During my first trip into the kitchen, I looked down at my feet. There was a pet food bowl. I was puzzled. I knew that Pete and Carol didn't have a pet. I picked it up. It was a little ceramic bowl that had been personalized with a name painted on one side: Freddie.

Pete smiled sheepishly when I asked him about the dish after their return. "Well, he kind of grew on us," he said, chuckling. "I guess it's because Freddie just doesn't seem like a cat. He reminds me of a dog, a wonderful dog."

They sent Freddie Christmas cards and gave him little gifts. And sometimes Pete would call us, saying, "I've had a hard day at work. I need a Freddie fix. Could you hand him over the fence?" And we would.

When a few years later Pete was dying of bladder cancer, Freddie was there with him, cuddled next to him in bed, day after day, giving comfort and warmth to his anguished days and nights.

This comfort wasn't without a price. When we noticed that Freddie was suddenly lethargic, even for a cat (which we defined as lying down twice on the way to his food bowl at dinnertime), we rushed him to Dr. Tracy. After running lab tests and doing a thorough physical and finding no trace of disease, she looked closely into his eyes.

"This kitty is depressed," she said at last. "Has he had a significant loss lately? He seems to be grieving."

Freddie grieved anew some months after Pete's death when Pete's widow, Carol, died in a catastrophic house fire, caused by faulty electrical wiring that gutted her home and damaged ours. The day after the fire, Freddie spent hours next door, sifting among the ruins, before he came home, covered with ashes, and lay face down on the bed, overwhelmed.

Now, three years later, Freddie was dying of cancer. It had started with a spot on his nose that Dr. Tracy had excised. When the cancer recurred two years later, Dr. Tracy spent a lunch hour personally driving Freddie to a veterinarian friend's practice where he could get more advanced laser surgery.

I was in awe of her willingness to make a forty-mile round trip with a cat whose extreme yowling and thrashings during car rides had prompted us to choose vets based on which one was half a block closer—until Dr. Tracy had opened her Cat Doctor practice near our home.

"Oh, it was a pleasure," Dr. Tracy said, laughing, of her vehicular adventure with Freddie. "He sang all the way. See, if you reframe it as singing, it isn't so bad!"

Despite Dr. Tracy's loving care, the cancer came back, and it spread with a vengeance, destroying Freddie's nose, upper lip, and palate.

Even with the disintegration of his face, Freddie lived his life as he always had—visiting neighborhood friends, eating with gusto, cuddling as readily as ever. We were devastated at the prospect of losing him, especially Bob, as he reflected on the countless times that Freddie had helped pull him through epilepsy-related emotional crises by his gentle presence and his loving touch. And so we dedicated ourselves to giving Freddie the best quality of life for as long as possible, keeping him hydrated with daily saline infusions. Freddie would settle comfortably into Bob's lap, looking at him with love and trust as Bob slid the needle between his shoulder blades for that day's infusion. "You'll know when it's time to let go," Dr. Tracy had told us. "He'll let you know. But, in the meantime, he's enjoying his life."

The two tiny kittens mewed for my attention. I turned around. One of them was a fluffy red tabby. The other was sleek, cream-colored with a hint of red tabby markings. They had been curled up together when I had walked in but were now pressed up against the bars of their cage, their paws extended, and purring loudly. They looked like little lion cubs. The light one met my eyes and held the gaze.

"No, Sweetheart," I said softly, more to myself than to the kittens. "We have a very sick kitty who needs our full attention. We aren't looking for kittens just now."

I turned away as the receptionist came back with our supply of saline for the week. The kittens mewed. I spun around. They were still pressing against the bars of their cage and reaching toward me. The light one looked into my eyes again and stood perfectly still, his gaze unwavering. The red tabby started purring.

The receptionist smiled. "Aren't they adorable?" she said.

I couldn't stop looking at them, reaching out, mewing, wanting to be touched and held. "Tell me about these kittens," I said at last.

They were the last two of a litter of five kittens crammed into a small box and dumped in a local junkyard when they were only two to three weeks old. That was in July, and the Southern California summer was a blazing one. When a passing postal carrier heard their faint cries they were near death. He took one look into the box and rushed them to Dr. Tracy. She and her staff spent a month nursing the five kittens back to health, hand-feeding them and playing with them as they grew.

Now it was late August. They were eight weeks old and healthy, and it was time to find homes for them. Three of the kittens—two red tabbies and a calico—had already been adopted. These were the last two. And there was a problem, she said. These two had such a strong emotional bond with each other that Dr. Tracy was insisting that they be adopted together. Many had expressed interest in the red tabby—whom they had named "Big Red"—but nobody wanted "Blondie," the light one.

Part of the problem was that Big Red was a beautiful, fluffy red tabby with soulful eyes and a gentle manner. Blondie, who looked to be getting the worse part of the genetic deal, appeared to be a mixture of red tabby and Burmese. He was neither beautiful nor mellow. Blondie was an awkward combination, with a tabby face and skinny Burmese tail. And he was vocal, demanding attention. Even when he was quiet, an intensity lingered.

I looked at him once again and he looked back, not moving. And the receptionist told me that there was another problem: this little one had a medical condition—a heart defect that might correct itself within the first year. But if it didn't, he was likely to die within the next few years. And no one wanted a little kitten who could die. The red tabby began to groom his little brother as Blondie still stared into my eyes.

It was insane. We didn't need kittens just now, especially one with special medical needs. We needed to focus on our beloved and dying elderly cat. Yet Blondie's gaze was unwavering. I began to feel an aching, fiercely loving bond with both of them. My eyes filled with tears, and I grabbed my cell phone, dialing our home number.

When my husband, Bob, answered, and I begged him to come see these kittens, he was aghast. What was I thinking?

"I know," I said, fighting tears. "It's totally insane. But we have to adopt these kittens. I can't begin to explain. You just have to see them."

Minutes later, Bob walked into Dr. Tracy's lobby, took one look at them, and fell in love. Gently, he lifted Blondie out of the cage. The kitten rubbed his cheek against Bob's, then rested his head on Bob's shoulder, purring loudly.

"That little one has fought so hard to live in the past month," Dr. Tracy said, coming to the lobby with a departing client. "He's the runt of the litter. His fight isn't over. His heart may or may not heal itself. And if it doesn't within the next year, he'll probably die suddenly."

Bob kissed the purring kitten and tightened his embrace. "It doesn't matter," he said, his eyes filling with tears. "Even if he dies soon, no matter how short or long his life is, I want every day of his life to be filled with love and happiness." The kitten purred and rubbed his furry cheek against Bob's, catching a falling tear. "And I'm going to name him Timmy, the sweetest name I know. We'll take them both."

I smiled with a mixture of relief and amusement. I was so glad that Bob agreed that we adopt these kittens. And the name was a fun surprise. We had never discussed naming a cat "Timmy" before. But when Bob saw Blondie with those intelligent eyes and affectionate, warm manner, the name seemed to fit. Was he thinking of Tim Schellhardt, a noted journalist, one of my best friends from college and a dear friend to Bob as well, who had these same qualities? Or was Timmy named after the sweet-faced boy with a penchant for falling down wells on *Lassie*? Bob shrugged when I asked him. "It just came to me," he said. "It just seemed to be exactly the right name for that little kitten."

And so we returned home, with the week's saline and two kittens, to an elderly cat who barely registered surprise when he saw the additions to the family. Freddie had a warm spot for kittens, and these were no exception. But when it dawned on him that they were not visiting, but staying, he decided to ignore them.

For several days, we cuddled the kittens while Freddie made his neighborhood rounds. Later on, we'd put the kittens to bed in our second bathroom so that we could give Freddie our undivided attention. Gradually, his "If I don't look at them, they're not there" mindset faded. They were family.

As in any family, there were inevitable squabbles. Freddie found lively, curious Timmy a trial, especially when Timmy pounced on his painfully protruding spine, ambushing him as he walked by the living room couch. Freddie's weight had dropped from a robust eighteen pounds to barely five pounds in the eight months of his illness. He wasn't in the mood for wrestling with a rambunctious kitten.

But Freddie and Big Red, whom we had renamed Gus, bonded quickly. Gus was a quiet, thoughtful little kitten who lived to nurture—his brother, Freddie, his humans. He climbed quickly into Bob's lap as Bob struggled with epilepsy-related mood swings. Bob has temporal lobe epilepsy, one of the features of which can be cyclical bouts of deep, immobilizing depression that has no connection to life events. Gus seemed to recognize immediately that there were times when Bob needed loving attention. Gus was also attentive to his beloved brother, holding him in his paws all day when Timmy remained groggy from the anesthetic after both kittens were neutered. And he adored Freddie, following him around, grooming him when Freddie lost the ability to groom himself, sharing meals with him. And, as Freddie lay dying at the end of our bed, shivering with a chill only he could feel, Gus snuggled up beside him, trying to warm and comfort him as Timmy dashed around on the floor below, indulging in typical crazy kitten antics.

Although Freddie never really did let us know that he was ready to go—living life fully right up to the end, continuing to eat enthusiastically and visiting neighborhood friends the last day of his life—we could see the end approaching. We saw it when he cried out in pain suddenly as I touched his stomach while bathing him. We saw it when he wandered the house in a daze, mistaking the laundry basket for the litter box. We saw it in the increasing time Freddie spent shivering on the bed, burying his face in Gus' soft fur. And one day in late October, with a quick injection from Dr. Tracy while resting in Bob's arms, Freddie gently slipped away.

We were stunned by the waves of grief that followed. Both Bob and I cried as much over the loss of Freddie as we had cried over our parents' deaths. Bob held Freddie's favorite red rhinestone collar and wept. He curled up on the couch with Freddie's urn and sobbed. I found myself near tears many times a day and crying in the shower as I had done so often when my parents died. Though we managed to contain our grief at work, our evenings were tearful, lightened only by the presence of Timmy and Gus, who needed to be cared for and loved—and who gave so much in return.

Even as we grieved Freddie's death, we rejoiced in Timmy's healthy new life. At six months, he showed no sign of his previous heart ailment. He was growing, thriving, and vibrantly alive. The sight of him racing around the house with his favorite ribbon or his constant presence and interest in everything we did kept us smiling through our tears.

Although they remained close and loving with each other as they grew into young cats, the differences between Timmy and Gus became increasingly apparent with time. Timmy's physical being was an uneasy mix of red tabby and Burmese. "His mother was a slut!" Dr. Tracy joked during his six-month checkup. "He and Gus obviously had different fathers."

Even though his health had improved, Timmy was still not a beautiful cat.

He had the short, fine, cream-colored hair of a Burmese, the sleek body lines of the breed, and a hint of his red tabby heritage in faint body and face markings, including two red markings that looked like little eyebrows over his wide brown eyes. His little body was inflexible for a cat's and he had the density of a Burmese—feeling much heavier than he looked, especially if he happened to be standing on one's lap with his tiny but painfully heavy feet. He also had the skinny tail characteristic of Asian breeds.

His brother Gus was undeniably beautiful—with deep red tabby markings, a highly flexible body, soulful green eyes, and a lush tail.

But something about Timmy always prompted a double take. For all his physical shortcomings, something in his eyes held attention and spoke of mystery and the fact that he was a sentient being.

He was complicated and highly intelligent, showing emotions like jealousy and guilt. He talked back vigorously when scolded and enjoyed carrying on conversations—in a fascinating pattern of repetitive and unique sounds—nearly constantly with Bob. He basked in attention. While Gus would always alert us if Timmy got accidentally trapped in our bedroom closet, Timmy would never do the same for Gus. He was happy to have our undivided attention until Gus' howls alerted us to his situation.

Timmy had a variety of obsessions. One was a red ribbon from a Christmas gift I had received when he was a kitten. For years, he dragged that ribbon around the house and my office, inviting anyone he encountered to seize the ribbon and run with it while he gave chase.

He was also obsessed with dental floss. No matter how carefully and silently Bob would open the floss container, no matter what part of the house Timmy happened to be in at that moment, in another instant he would be on Bob's chest, his head in Bob's mouth, snapping at the floss. They had a routine: after Bob flossed his own teeth, he would floss Timmy's, letting him bite the floss while keeping a firm grip on it and finally flushing it down the toilet to keep Timmy from raiding the wastebasket.

Another obsession was my sister's—only my sister's—hair. Timmy loved to chew on my sister Tai's long hair when she visited. A confirmed cat lover who has always had multiple cats of her own, she was, nonetheless, prone to Timmy-fatigue after several nights of his cuddling up to her in bed, licking and chewing her hair through the night.

But it was Timmy's faults and shortcomings as much as his joyous, outgoing nature that made him special to us—at least as special as his brother Gus.

Gus is a beautiful, sweet cat who delights in nurturing: first his brother, then us, and later a succession of kittens who joined our family at various times. He has never bitten or scratched. He has no obsessions, no special demands, no annoying habits. He asks very little. He just wants to love and be loved, dropping to the floor at one's feet, purring in anticipation of petting and attention.

Although, as they grew, Gus seemed the more loving and sensitive cat, Timmy's outgoing nature blossomed. He loved people—everyone, anyone who came in the door. Sometimes, his enthusiasm was a shock.

"Isn't he supposed to do the cat thing and hide under the bed when guests come?" asked one faintly cat-phobic friend, recoiling as Timmy jumped to the top of her chair and began roiling around in her long, thick hair.

"Get him away from me!" another friend screamed when Timmy, without warning, jumped on his shoulder and clung there, purring, as our friend flailed his arms wildly.

As time went on, Timmy retained his enthusiasm for people but learned a bit more restraint. He stopped terrorizing guests, though he liked to be a part of company visits. But he was increasingly low-key. He would check out guests, hungry for attention, but he would often wander off after a short time, cuddling on our bed with his brother. Gus, cautious and wary of strangers, would rarely appear to greet company.

But both Timmy and Gus were wonderful with Bob, whether he was suffering a grand mal seizure, whether he was experiencing a depressive episode, or whether he was in a cycle of nightmares and night terrors—all related to his epilepsy.

The nights when Bob woke screaming from nightmares and suffered night terrors were stressful and sleepless for both of us—until we began to get some feline interventions.

When Bob would awaken at night, groaning and screaming, Gus would come running. Leaping on Bob's chest, he would lie down on him, nuzzling his face and purring loudly. Bob invariably calmed down and often fell soundly asleep.

Both Timmy and Gus seemed to sense when Bob's depression was back. Gus would climb onto his lap, embrace him with his paws, and purr, sometimes for hours. Timmy always took his special place at Bob's shoulder, perching there and talking to him in a soft little murmur, now and then rubbing Bob's cheek with his own until Bob's mood lightened.

Timmy followed Bob everywhere, watchful, adoring. They played together, napped together, and meditated together. Bob had always considered Freddie to be the ultimate companion cat, and, in many ways, this was true. Freddie had spent hours lying in Bob's lap, sharing the good times and consoling him through the dark times. But Timmy and Gus were proving to be wonderfully therapeutic in their own special ways.

"My little therapists!" Bob would say, smiling at last. "We had no idea, did we? Who knew how much we really *did* need these kittens?"

Two:

A MOMENT THAT CHANGED EVERYTHING

"Please, I'm desperate!" The voice on the phone was punctuated with sobs. "I know you're moving offices this week and weren't planning to see patients. But this is urgent. I really, really need to see you!"

I sighed. The only available office space I had that weekend of transition was my separate home office, which I used for writing. I had never used it for patients. While some therapists do use attached or detached home offices with separate entrances to see patients, I wasn't crazy about the idea. There were some patients I would not want to know what city I lived in, let alone the exact location. I felt most comfortable keeping my professional and personal lives quite separate.

But this was Julia, the patient I had been seeing longer—at that point—than any other. She had, in fact, been my very first patient at my first internship, five years before. Then she had been a college student planning to drop out of school in her sophomore year. Now she was a proud graduate, excelling in her first job but struggling intermittently with a major love relationship. Julia had followed me every time I had changed internship sites and into my private practice once I was, at long last, a licensed therapist. We had been through a lot together, Julia and I.

I took a deep breath and made a quick decision. "Would you feel comfortable coming to my house, Julia?" I asked. "I could meet with you in my home office today. Bob is gone all day with his volunteer work. It would just be us—and, of course, the kitties."

She laughed through her tears. "The kitties," she said. "Oh, this is my chance to meet your cats! It would be perfect! Thank you!"

Two hours later, she was on my doorstep. At the first sight of her, Gus ran for the bedroom and slid under the bed. Timmy came up to greet her, then followed his brother into the bedroom, curling up on the bed.

Since we were alone and she was in such distress, I invited Julia to sit down immediately on the living room couch and tell me what was going on.

She shook her head, unable to speak through her sobs.

Suddenly, a flash of white streaked past me and onto her lap. It was Timmy. He stood on her lap, wiping her tears with a soft paw and rubbing her face with his furry cheek. Then he curled back down onto her lap, purring loudly.

Julia began to pet him, calming enough to speak at last. She looked up from Timmy and said, "You know, if you had something else you needed to be doing just now, Timmy and I will be fine here. Seriously, can this kitty join us for all my sessions?"

As intrigued as I was with Julia's request to include Timmy in her sessions, I hesitated.

Although animal-assisted therapy has been catching on in recent years—with dogs, horses, and sometimes even cats—working with populations from autistic kids to the bedridden elderly in nursing homes, I hadn't considered using it in my private psychotherapy practice.

This wasn't because I was a stranger to clinical improvisation.

In fact, I had spent much of my life improvising my way through challenging situations—from a childhood where I dealt with an alcoholic, mentally ill father who was both loving and abusive, to my decades of work as a journalist and stories that had brought me into contact with people going through emotional high and low points in their lives, to my decision in midlife to return to graduate school to become a psychotherapist.

Through clinical internships and then my professional experience as a therapist, I had learned a great deal about working with patients. Classroom lessons, often rooted largely in psychoanalytic and psychodynamic techniques, were useless when working with court-ordered patients or otherwise nontraditional, disadvantaged clients who tended to respond better to more practical cognitive-behavioral techniques. In my internship at a gritty urban clinic with a large population of court-ordered and low-income clients, I quickly learned the importance of flexibility and innovation.

After I was fully licensed as a therapist, I split my time between my growing suburban private practice and work at a large urban psychiatric clinic specializing in treating patients whose lives had been forever changed by disabling, sometimes eventually fatal work-related injuries.

My clinic patients were a rainbow of diversity—in terms of ethnicity, life experience, and occupation. Many would never have set foot in a psychiatric clinic but for a devastating physical injury. They came from factories, banks, retail outlets, and government offices, and two of them were from the San Fernando Valley's burgeoning porn film industry. There were huge cultural considerations and some language barriers. Two of my longtime clients communicated through medical interpreters.

Through all of these experiences—in the clinics of my internships and later as a licensed therapist with injured workers at this psychiatric clinic—I learned that there are times when you throw away the notion of traditional therapy and do what works. It may mean taking an outstretched hand. It may mean confronting a scary new patient who is throwing chairs in the waiting room with a question like "What's frightening you so much?" and squeezing her hand as her face crumples and the tears flow. It may mean joking with someone who needs to laugh as well as to cry. It may mean embracing a frightened patient with a life-threatening injury who is begging to be held.

So trying my hand at animal-assisted therapy in my private practice should not have been a stretch.

Still, I hesitated.

I had viewed my suburban private practice as a bastion of traditional therapy—with patients who had insurance and reasonably stable lives, patients whose depression, anxiety, marital issues, and surly teenagers were the more or less typical clinical scenario most would-be therapists imagine in graduate school. I had been reluctant to stray too far from what I considered to be the therapeutic norm.

And it had simply never occurred to me that an animal that brought so much comfort to me and to Bob at home could reach out to others in a professional setting.

True, I had read the studies about the benefits of animal contact. There was the scientific study demonstrating that the sound frequencies in the range of a cat's purr could promote healing and improve bone density. There were numerous studies showing a positive association between having a pet and lower blood pressure, heart rate, and cholesterol. Other studies found that companion animals could decrease loneliness and enhance one's sense of well-being. And one study of 4,000 subjects found that spending time with a cat could be so comforting—reducing anxiety levels to such an extent—that heart attack rates were lowered by as much as one-third.

But I hadn't imagined involving Timmy in therapy work. As I thought about it then, I couldn't help but worry that it might be asking too much of him.

Even though Timmy was healthy, loved people, and was reliably friendly and calm under stressful circumstances, I worried. In a very real sense, being a therapy cat would be nothing new to him, yet I wondered if being with relative strangers in distress might prove too stressful. I watched him purring on Julia's lap. He seemed fine. Maybe he would just work with Julia. Or maybe just a few patients. It might be worth a try.

Then there were the logistics: How does one use a therapy animal with some patients but protect others who may have allergies or phobias?

My solution was to make Saturday, the only day Julia was able to come to therapy, our therapy cat day. All of the clients who wanted to work with Timmy would need to reschedule for Saturday. I carefully screened my other clients on that day for allergies or cat phobia, giving them the option to reschedule for another day or evening if necessary. And the one Saturday patient who was allergic to cats and could not reschedule would always be my first client of the day—with Timmy confined securely in the adjacent bathroom.

There were practical considerations as well, such as checking with building management to make sure having an animal in the building didn't violate any of their rules and checking with my liability and malpractice insurance carrier to make sure this type of therapy would be covered.

I made the decision to keep animal-assisted therapy very informal and cost-free. Many of the patients Timmy saw were referred and approved by insurance companies for psychotherapy for a certain standard rate. A few were private pay. But for all, Timmy's services were at no additional cost and on an as-needed basis. With some clients, he was always present; with others, just initially; and with still others, only at times when they were feeling unusually anxious or depressed.

Timmy started working with Julia immediately. I put his picture on the bulletin board of my office, offering Saturday sessions of animal-assisted therapy to anyone who was interested.

While only a small number of patients chose to try working with Timmy, most of the others were intrigued with the idea and loved seeing his picture. Some asked, "So is Timmy going to take over some of your patients?" or "Is this like just being in a room with a cat and petting it and feeling better?"

The answers to these questions were "No" and "Maybe."

The therapy animal doesn't replace the human therapist but helps patients who may be too anxious or depressed to talk readily to relax to the point that therapeutic talk is possible.

Sometimes petting a cat helps a patient to relax. For others, just being in a room with a friendly animal nearby helps to soothe anxiety. For still others, engaging in play with an animal can help them to create some relief and some temporary distance from issues that are difficult to address immediately or for sustained periods of time. And for some couples or families in conflict, an affectionate, playful animal can distract them from the fury of their conflict long enough to let them cool down and begin to talk with each other in a way that makes understanding and compromise possible.

Timmy did all of the above. He had an uncanny sense about what sort of feline intervention might work best: whether to snuggle and purr, to play, or simply to sit nearby, reassuring the patient with his warm presence.

In all ways, it was a continuation of the joy that he and Gus and Freddie had inspired at home so many times.

In a new role that began when he rushed to comfort Julia, Timmy approached our work together with his typical enthusiasm. He helped Julia to trust again and an elderly widow to feel hope. He helped to bridge the silence with a troubled teenager and inspired a newly divorced client to smile for the first time in months. He helped to decrease the anger and defensiveness of a client—without even being in the room with her initially.

In short, Timmy touched and changed some lives—some for a moment or long enough to begin to resolve a crisis or a problem. He changed my life—as a therapist and as a cat lover—forever.

And it all began with Julia.

Three:

TIMMY, THE THERAPY CAT

Timmy and Julia: Healing by Feeling That You Matter

Julia's eyes sparkled when she saw him. "Timmy!" she cried as he rushed into her arms. "Has it been only a week since we've seen each other? How are you, my little buddy?" She buried her face in his fur.

I sat back, enjoying this moment of warm connection between the two. I had seen Julia through several phases of healing in my years of work with her. Now she seemed to be entering another phase of growth, aided by her warm connection with Timmy.

I had first met Julia five years before when she was assigned to me as my very first patient in my first clinical internship.

It had seemed, at least initially, to be an unfortunate pairing. I had asked specifically that I not be assigned any clients with an eating disorder until I was more experienced as a therapist. At the time, I was struggling with my own eating disorder and weighed more than 250 pounds, making me an anorexic or bulimic patient's worst nightmare. Julia's records stated that she had suffered bulimia with four hospitalizations.

But the clinic director sighed and explained to me that Julia had seen every one of my fellow interns already and that none of the therapeutic relationships had worked out. As awkward a match as I might be, I was her last chance at this facility.

Julia quickly looked me up and down when I walked out into the waiting room to greet her but said nothing. She was even more nervous than I in our first session, repeatedly slapping her own cheeks and telling herself softly to "Calm down, Julia! Calm down!" while jumping from chair to chair in the four-patient seating arrangement in the room. I stayed as still as possible those first few minutes, both to hide my own nervousness and to give an illusion of calm that I hoped would be contagious. Julia began to calm down and talk. She thanked me cheerfully at the end of the session, careful to schedule our next meeting before she left. She showed up for our second session, looking eager and bringing her diary to discuss with me. I was feeling encouraged.

But just before our third session, my supervisor insisted that I bring up the issue of my weight. I felt that if it hadn't come up in a session already, I would leave it alone. My supervisor, a slender Beverly Hills psychotherapist with a relentlessly psychoanalytic orientation, shook her head. "It may just be the—excuse the expression—elephant in the room," she said, pursing her lips and looking at me with faint disapproval. "I want you to do the session in the room with the one-way window, and I'll observe."

I was cornered. Julia and I would be spending our third session in the dreaded one-way observation window room where all interns had to work with a client under direct, unseen supervision at least once a month. Due to her therapeutic misadventures with other interns at this facility, Julia had spent a lot of time in this one-way-mirror room. When I told her that this session would be observed, she simply shrugged and sighed, "Whatever."

Early on in the session, I asked Julia how it was for her to have a therapist who was significantly overweight. She squinted at me, puzzled. "Did your supervisor tell you to bring that up?" she asked, aware that we were being observed. "You're not that overweight. I hardly noticed, truly."

Suddenly facing the one-way window and addressing my unseen supervisor, Julia added, "I don't have an issue with my therapist's weight at all! I'm in recovery with bulimia. It hasn't been a problem for several years. I'm here because of school problems and my anger problem with my boyfriend. Okay? And she's helping me a lot!"

And so we continued on together over the years of my training and beyond. When I would switch internships, Julia would follow me to a new one. When I got my psychotherapy license and started a private practice, Julia was there.

But she still struggled at times.

Julia was generally a quiet, depressed young woman who had felt rejected her whole life: by a father who left her behind both physically and emotionally when her parents divorced during her toddler years, and by a mother who didn't know how to love this daughter who had come as a midlife surprise. Although her eating disorder remained in remission, she was still self-critical, bemoaning the fact that she was so tall. She couldn't see the physical beauty that was so apparent to others: her lovely, sweet face; her healthy, svelte body; her innate sense of style. She was quick to label herself as "crazy" as she struggled with her fears and insecurities. She could also be critical and volatile with others: Julia's relationship with her boyfriend, Jake, still could be tempestuous. She could go from mild irritation to threats of breaking up forever in a matter of seconds. Her friendships, except for a precious few, proved fragile. Julia was reserved, anticipating endings rather than beginnings, rejection rather than acceptance.

Yet here she was with Timmy, cuddling and laughing with delight. Timmy rubbed his cheek against her hand, looked into her eyes, and purred loudly.

"I love you, Timmy," she whispered. "You're the best!"

Cradled in her arms, Timmy rested and purred, his eyes never leaving her face.

She spoke quietly and with wonder. "I think he likes me," she said.

"Does that surprise you?"

"Yes," she said. "I don't think most people do when they first meet me or even after they get to know me. It's hard to say. I don't trust people most of the time. But animals don't lie, do they? I mean, if they like you, they show it, and, if they don't, I guess they just sort of avoid you, right?"

"You're thinking that if Timmy likes you so much right away . . ."

"It means I have to have something going for me." She looked at me, a trace of hope in her suddenly tear-filled eyes. She hugged Timmy tightly. He closed his eyes and continued to purr.

"What are your tears saying that you can't right now?"

"That I matter."

And so we went on through weeks and months together, Julia, Timmy, and I. Although there were no instant miracles, there were more hopeful moments as Julia, soothed by Timmy's presence, grew in her insights into her own life, feelings, and behavior: how she was quick to reject others before they could reject her; how she grieved the loving parenting she had never had growing up, with unrealistic expectations that teachers and employers would step in as parent figures; how the hurtful comments she hurled at Jake mirrored her lifelong pain within. It wasn't an easy time for the three of us, but Timmy hung in there at least as tenaciously as Julia and I had over the years.

Every time Julia arrived, Timmy greeted her with a warm cuddle. As she embraced him, she marveled at how enduring their relationship had turned out to be. No matter how agitated she might get, no matter how loud her crying, Timmy stayed close.

"Just think about how loving you are with him," I suggested. "You embrace him whether you're having a good day or really bad day. Is that different in any way from some of your close relationships with the humans in your life?"

Julia paused. Her wide blue eyes lingered over Timmy's upturned face as she tenderly stroked his throat. "Yes," she said at last. "I don't accept love as easily from humans. I'm afraid they'll leave me, so I demand proof of love by . . . what? I act like a brat and then hope they'll stay. I don't say loving things, just critical things. I guess I want to know that a person would love me no matter what. With Timmy, I just accept him as he is, this minute. Is that what I should be doing with Jake? Or a friend? Just this?"

"Well, it might be worth a try, just to see what happens," I said.

"But . . ." Julia looked doubtful. "Sometimes Jake is an awful jerk, you know."

I nodded. Jake had come into therapy with Julia on occasion, clearly showing both his strengths as a partner and the challenges he brought to the relationship. They had both smiled at the last session, anticipating my directives. "Yes," they said in unison. "We know. We need to treat each other nicely, tenderly, and with respect. And we're really trying."

"I know you're both trying hard to improve your relationship," I said. "Just remember that no one is perfect, but you can choose to love through conflict and pain."

She hugged Timmy and considered her options. "It's worth a try," she said at last. "I'll hug Jake just like he was Timmy!"

The warmth of her relationship with Timmy encouraged her to take the risk of reaching out to another with love instead of drawing back and sabotaging a relationship before she could be hurt. She tried this numerous times with Jake. She tried it with her longtime friend Sylvie, who had told Julia previously that she found their friendship both rewarding and terribly stressful. Julia was amazed when her love was met by love in return.

She smiled as she reported that her relationship with Jake was improving, that when she treated him with tenderness, he responded in kind. Then one day she arrived with a sparkling engagement ring on her finger.

"Who knew that could happen . . . for me?" she said with a hint of wonder in her voice. "But Timmy knew. He knew right away—that I'm a loving person."

And she held him close once more.

Julia clung to Timmy in all the turmoil and excitement of her first year of marriage, as our sessions continued. She reported that her relationship with Jake was improving steadily, that her backsliding into angry threats had stopped. She began to envision the two of them as a real family and hoped that they would be adding a child or two to this family soon. She was calmer, more self-accepting; her face shone with happiness.

And it was time—at long last—to say good-bye. Life was good and changing in a variety of ways. She and Jake had good jobs lined up and were relocating out of state. The day we sat down for our last session, it had been more than six years since our initial meeting. The nervous college kid was now a calm, self-accepting, happy woman. I had changed, too: from a nervous intern to a seasoned, licensed psychotherapist. But though I no longer weighed what I had when we first met, I was still significantly overweight.

As the end of the session neared, Julia said that there was something else she wanted to tell me. Her eyes filled with tears. "I did notice how overweight you were when we first met, even though I minimized it when your supervisor insisted that you bring it up in our session," she said. "I didn't want to hurt your feelings. I've always loved working with you, right from that first day. But I just want to say, now that I'm leaving, that I hope you continue to lose weight and to take care of yourself as wonderfully as you've taken care of me. Because I love you and I want you to live a long and healthy, happy life."

With Timmy squeezed, purring, between us, Julia and I embraced.

Timmy and Peter: Rediscovering the Value of Fun

Peter came to therapy suffering what he described as "an emotional double whammy": his four-year-old fourth marriage had collapsed when his wife left him for her high school sweetheart after reconnecting with her old flame at their tenth high school reunion. Shortly thereafter, Alex, his beloved fourteen-year-old black Lab, had died.

A handsome television producer, Peter's sandy blond hair and tall, slim, but well-muscled body made him look considerably younger than his forty-eight years. Youth was a big deal for Peter—both in terms of looking young and having a lovely young woman on his arm. His penchant for beautiful young women who turned out to be more interested in his power and money than in him had brought him no end of pain and had cost him a small fortune besides. Peter worked long hours, and even his recreation was work. Whether at the gym or relaxing over drinks with friends, he was alert, watching, hoping to find just the right contact or talent or arm candy any minute.

But now Peter was overwhelmed with grief, depression, and a sense of failure, feeling too exhausted and discouraged to imagine building a new life for himself.

His mood improved somewhat during our first few months of sessions, but he still felt that life was drudgery, filled with unending effort and few rewards. His social life was dwindling, and his work was beginning to feel tedious. He told me that he knew that therapy was hard work, too, but that he was beginning to feel overwhelmed with all he needed to do to heal his pain and find more joy in living.

His eyes lit up when he spotted Timmy's picture and an announcement on my office bulletin board that I was offering animal-assisted therapy. Suddenly intrigued, Peter asked about Timmy and how animal-assisted therapy worked. Despite his interest, he was nevertheless skeptical.

"I'm not such a cat person," he said. "But I miss the feel of Alex, just petting and holding him. I miss that warm creature who loved me no matter what. I miss . . ."

His eyes filled with tears. "I miss . . . so much!"

He decided to give Timmy a try but admitted some anxiety before their first session.

"How do I approach a cat?" he asked. "What am I supposed to do?"

"Just stop worrying and just sit quietly, take some deep breaths, and relax," I suggested. "Don't even think about Timmy or how things ought to be. Just be."

He closed his eyes, breathing slowly in and out, as I brought Timmy into the room. Timmy sat and watched him for a while. Peter opened his eyes and looked across the room at Timmy.

"He looks right in my eyes," he said. "I didn't think cats did that. It reminds me . . ."

And he talked and cried about Alex, whom he had adopted as a puppy when he first moved to Los Angeles from New York. He remembered what fun they used to have in their fourteen years together. Alex, in fact, had turned out to be his most faithful companion, outlasting all four of Peter's brief marriages. Peter delighted in pointing out the parallels between Alex and Timmy: how Alex had loved to romp and play; how Alex understood, without words, what he was feeling—just like Timmy. He looked at Timmy, unsure what to do next.

Suddenly Timmy grabbed his well-worn red ribbon and began running around the room with it, tossing it in the air and jumping and catching it in his mouth. When he saw Peter smile, he ran around in circles, finally falling and rolling around with the ribbon.

Peter slipped to the floor. "You really like that ribbon, don't you, buddy?" he said softly. "Can I have that ribbon? Can I?" He grabbed the ribbon and was on his feet, laughing and walking briskly around the room, trailing the ribbon, with Timmy at his heels.

Finally, he collapsed on the couch, smiling as he watched Timmy roll around with his reclaimed ribbon. With the ribbon in his mouth, Timmy jumped up on the couch beside Peter, looking happy and expectant.

"You want to play some more?" Peter asked him and then turned to me. "He reminds me of a dog. Alex never wanted to stop once we started playing. This one is the same." They made another few circles around the office, Timmy chasing Peter, Peter chasing Timmy. The next time Peter sat down, Timmy hopped onto his lap.

Peter already seemed lighter, happier.

Peter petted Timmy tentatively at first, gaining the confidence to hug him as the minutes went by. "It feels so good to hug a loving animal again," Peter said at last.

"It's a little different with each animal," I said. "But the love and warmth are the same. When you hug Timmy, what do you imagine? What do you hope for?"

Peter looked wistful.

"To love again, maybe get another dog when I feel ready," he said. "Maybe get serious about selling the house, giving my ex her share and buying a place of my own, maybe with a little yard or a park nearby. Something good for a dog. When I feel ready . . ."

Through the months to come, Peter talked and cried, often with Timmy in his arms or at his heels in pursuit of the red ribbon, and all the while we explored just what he needed to do to feel ready, to feel open to begin his life anew.

His progress was evident when he reported feeling younger within.

"I'm feeling younger at heart!" he announced one day several months into the sessions with Timmy, panting slightly after a run around the office with Timmy and his red ribbon.

Peter leaned back on the couch and stared at the ceiling, reflecting. "You know, feeling young within feels like . . . an infusion of happiness, of just letting go and laughing. It isn't so much about all my efforts to look younger or to have all of those young girlfriends and wives, all that pretending that I was young and rich or all the pretending that they cared about me. It's about being happy right here, right now, in this moment, romping with Timmy or talking plainly, without bullshitting, to you. I'm starting to feel lighter, more hopeful, that life can get better, maybe better than it ever was before."

He stopped, momentarily embarrassed by this flash of optimism. "It probably sounds stupid," he said. "It's all so obvious. But it hasn't been to me. The business is just so youth-oriented, so viciously competitive, so concentrated on seeming, not being—on image rather than reality. I know what I need to feel ready for the rest of my life, and it isn't a new girlfriend. It's keeping that sense of my real and playful self even when I'm doing what I need to do in this business."

And so our work continued—with Timmy and his red ribbon—as the months went by. As Peter felt more confident about the real person he was growing to be, his Mr. Hollywood façade started to slip away and he began to make steps into his new life. His first move was to buy a modest but comfortable new home.

"It's the first house I've owned that has truly felt like home," he said, cuddling Timmy one day. "It isn't to impress anyone. My other homes were palaces for show, meant to impress others even as I struggled to pay for them. I can afford this house. I like it. It just feels right, and it has a nice grassy backyard, just right for a dog."

That dog came along a few months later: a lively little beagle from rescue that he named Jerry.

"And right now, life feels very complete with just me and Jerry. For once, I'm not in a hurry to have everything right now. I have fun back in my life . . . thanks to him." He nodded at Timmy and gave him a kiss on the top of his head. "Timmy helped me to remember how important it is to have fun, real fun, in your life."

Timmy and Brittney: Enduring Strength with Feeling Important

"Look," she said, glancing at me, sullen and heavy-lidded. "I don't mean this as anything against you or anything disrespectful, but this is such a fucking waste of time. I mean, it's my parents who are nuts, not me. I'm the only normal one in the family."

Brittney looked older than her twelve years, her wide gray eyes distant and sad, occasionally revealing, in a flash, the frightened, vulnerable child she was trying so hard to hide.

Over the crisp white blouse and navy plaid skirt of her parochial school uniform, she was wearing a long black sweater. Her blunt-cut black hair and air of world-weariness suggested an aspiring Goth. But right now, she was a lonely kid with well-bitten nails and a stubborn determination not to show the depth of her distress.

"I am the only normal one in the family," she repeated, kicking at a leg of the coffee table in front of her. "It isn't fair that I'm the one who has to come here."

"Sometimes that happens, Brittney," I said. "Sometimes the normal one ends up in therapy. Anything you want to tell me about what's going on at home and how our time together might help you to deal with that, I would like to hear. This is your time. How can we make the best use of it for you, so you don't have the frustration of thinking it's all such a waste?"

She thought for a moment. "I'd like to find a way to get my homework done so I can watch my favorite television shows at night."

"So let's talk about that. Let's figure out what's keeping you from doing that now and what might be changed."

She brightened—and we discussed her procrastination habit and her love of lists and goals. We came up with a simple but elegant plan that she told me the next week had helped a lot.

Then she lapsed into sullen silence again and avoided my eyes. "What if we take a walk and talk?" I asked her.

"Okay," she said without much enthusiasm. I had often had young clients open up much more readily when they could escape the pressures of the therapy room and not have to look at me directly when they talked. Walk therapy helped a little with Brittney. But she still guarded her family situation and her feelings about this closely and firmly.

Finally, I asked her if she would like to meet Timmy. She looked intrigued. "I always wanted a cat," she said wistfully. "But my parents wouldn't let me. Too much trouble, too much mess and clutter. Even though I said I'd take care of it, they wouldn't let me. You mean, I could pet a cat right here?" She smiled tentatively.

Brittney and Timmy bonded quickly. She loved petting him and marveled at his loud and constant purring.

"The funny thing about cats, at least some cats, is that you can talk to them and I really think they understand," I told her. "When I was growing up, we had a cat named Edie. And my younger sister, who had a time of really feeling down when she was in seventh grade, used to talk to Edie and tell her everything. What do you think about that?"

"It sounds a little crazy," she said. "But what the hell? Maybe Timmy would listen for a little while. You can stay if you want. But just remember, I'm talking to Timmy, okay?"

"Okay," I said. "But if I get curious and want to ask something, do you want me to ask Timmy or should I ask you directly?"

She was already cuddling him and rubbing her cheek against his. "Ask Timmy first," she said.

And she talked to him of many things: her feelings that she didn't matter in a household with two business executive parents who drank and fought too much and expressed their love too little; her fear that her parents might divorce and that neither would want to take her; that there was something wrong with her; that the only time she got attention was when she messed up, but she really didn't want to mess up at school or in life.

She wept into his fur as she held him. She locked eyes as she told him her greatest fears: that she would never be important to anyone, that she would always feel left out, that all her difficulties now were interfering with her schoolwork, and that she was feeling like a failure and was scared that it would always be this way. She sobbed that her parents expected her to fail, maybe wanted her to fail. And yet she feared that, even if she were to make all A's and graduate at the top of her class and win admittance to an Ivy League college, they would not be impressed and would turn things around so that she would fail despite all her hard work. Her parents seemed to have given up on her . . . or maybe they never, ever believed in her. And sometimes it was just so hard to keep telling herself that she could succeed, that everything would turn out well. Through it all, Timmy stayed close, not moving. He just listened, focused only on her.

As her confidence grew, Brittney began to assert herself more at home, asking her parents for encouragement and guidance, talking about her goals and plans for the future.

She told them when she aced a test. They shrugged and said, "Of course, that's what we expect of you. Why are you telling us this?"

She shared her dreams of attending a top-tier college and majoring in engineering as her father had years before. Now her father teased her about having such big dreams and suggested that she scale down to a nearby state school and study to become a teacher. Her mother simply shook her head at all the dreams shared and said that her dream was that Brittney would remember to do all her chores around the house. The more dismissive they became, the more insistent Brittney became to them that she wanted to achieve important goals in her life.

Her parents found this assertiveness and self-assurance unsettling and chose to remove her from therapy.

"But this has helped," she said at our last session. "It has helped to talk with Timmy. He made me feel so . . . important. And I'll never forget that. If I can just hang onto the idea that I am important and that, with enough work and effort, I can do amazing things, I'll be all right. I just know it." And she buried her face in Timmy's fur so that I wouldn't notice her tears.

Timmy and Linda: Self-Care for the Caregiver

Linda, a forty-three-year-old homemaker, mother of three children in middle school and high school and caregiver to her seventy-seven-year-old mother who was suffering from the early stages of dementia, described herself as "feeling squeezed and with advanced 'hurry up' syndrome. I'm always on the run and it never seems to be enough for anyone, including me. I keep thinking of what more I should be doing or how much better I could be doing it."

She sighed and sank into the chair. "I come last in my life and, right now, that can't be helped." She talked about her troubled relationship with her long-divorced mother who had been critical and distant all her life. Now her dementia was preventing her from living independently but was not so advanced that she had ceased to long for life as it used to be and she took her frustration out on Linda.

"Nothing I do pleases her," Linda said, twisting a tissue in her hands. "That's always been the case, but now it's worse because she's there with me twenty-four seven. And I have teenagers. I feel like I'm alternating between being constantly criticized and being pointedly ignored. There are times when my home doesn't seem like my home. My husband is being very patient about all this, but he gets to escape to work for hours every day. I'm stuck. Stuck with Mom. Stuck with my life . . ."

As stuck as she felt, Linda hesitated to speak about her feelings that came up as she dealt with her difficult mother and mouthy teenagers. But the feelings were there in her slender, restless body and the thinly veiled anger so evident in her eyes and in the firm set of her mouth. "I mean, sometimes I wonder what the point is in my coming here since there's nothing I can change about my life right now," she said. "My kids will still be teenagers. My mom will still be Mom."

I nodded. "It's true that you can't change some of these circumstances of your life," I said. "But perhaps we can explore ways you can approach and think about these circumstances, perhaps ways that you can feel more visible, more active, more supported in your busy life."

Linda was a restless client, getting up and pacing around or sitting with her hands and legs in constant motion. She had been in therapy for several weeks before she noticed my waiting-room bulletin board sign offering animal-assisted therapy and asked to try it "because I hope it will help me to kind of calm down a little. We used to have a dog who helped me to do that. And it was fun to take her out for walks, just the two of us. But she died a little over a year ago and, with Mom moving in, I don't know. . . . it just didn't seem to be the time to get another dog. There's so much to do now. I can't imagine one more thing, one more family member, to take care of."

When Timmy saw Linda for the first time, his response to her was immediate: he ran over and jumped on her lap and settled down for a nap.

A little surprised, more than a little uneasy, she stared at him. "What do I do now?" she asked.

"Just pet him or not . . . your choice," I said. "Maybe it would feel better just to sit there quietly with him on your lap."

"What if I want to get up and pace around?"

"You have a choice: you can lift him off your lap or ask him to get down, or you can stay still until he decides to move," I said.

She elected to stay still, petting him from time to time, and leaning back into the sofa cushions.

And it was then that the feelings spilled out: her resentment over her mother's refusal to spend three mornings a week at a special memory care program in order to give her outside stimulation and, not so incidentally, her daughter a bit of respite. "She has two long-time friends, people she knows there," Linda said, her exasperation evident. "But she just guilts me instead, like, 'You're just trying to get

rid of me. You don't care about me. All you care about is yourself!'
Ohh, as if . . ."

With Timmy there to soothe her, we talked about ways she could change her seemingly unchangeable life: from letting her teenagers know that all family members, including herself, needed to be treated with respect and that they were old enough to participate more fully in family chores and caregiving. She got strong backing from her husband, who also agreed to take on more caregiving and teen chauffeuring on weekends so that Linda could take the time to have a lunch with friends. She also was able to talk her mom into trying the memory care program for one day and then another with the suggestion, "Let's just see how this is for you. If you don't like it, okay. But it's a chance to see your friends and maybe get a little independence back."

Reluctantly at first, her mother agreed to go to memory day care for one day and then went back for a second day. Soon she was attending the program three days a week—sometimes enthusiastically, sometimes with a heavy sigh, but once there she always seemed glad to be with her two friends.

As time went on, Linda was noticeably less agitated. She cuddled comfortably and happily with Timmy, more at ease with him as time passed. There were times when she would fall into a contented silence, breathing deeply as she sat with him. Once she was so relaxed that she started to stretch her legs out and put her feet on the coffee table, before catching herself and apologizing.

"Just relax and put your feet up," I said. "This is a time just for you, when you can do what you want, no expectations, no judgments. . . ."

"It feels so good to sit here, just sit and relax and talk," Linda said. "I think that this is something I want to make time to do at home, maybe schedule like a standing appointment. Just take fifteen minutes or half an hour . . . just for me. I think it would help me to feel better about everything else."

"Let's talk about what this self-care would look like," I suggested.

Linda smiled at the thought. The frown lines between her eyebrows had been easing lately, and the anger was gone from her eyes. "Oh, I think I'd like to try meditating in the den with the doors closed," she said. "I'd like to read a magazine from cover to cover during a special time where no one is allowed to interrupt me. I'd like to take a walk for fresh air and a sense of freedom, even if for a few minutes. I'd like to have an uninterrupted twenty-minute phone visit with my best friend, Judy, once a week. I'd like . . . cuddling a little animal. . . ." She smiled down at Timmy.

"What would you think about getting another dog, maybe an adult rescue dog?" I asked. "Someone who could maybe sit on your lap and share this time out. Or someone to take on a walk, just the two of you . . ."

The thought made Linda smile as she relaxed with Timmy. She settled into the cushions and closed her eyes.

"Or maybe I'll get a rescue cat," she said at last, her eyes closed, a faint smile on her lips. "Cats are so . . . very . . . relaxing."

Timmy and Carly:
Facing Fears Equals Marital Bliss

C arly, referred by her medical doctor because of her constant anxiety and occasional panic attacks, flinched when she walked into my office and saw Timmy's picture on the bulletin board.

"You have a cat in here?" she asked, looking around frantically.

"Not today," I said. "Only on Saturdays. He works with a few of my clients."

"On what? How?" she asked, looking incredulous.

"Oh, he plays or sits on people's laps so they can pet him and feel better, sometimes less depressed, sometimes less anxious."

She took a deep breath. "I'm afraid of cats," she said. "I'm afraid of most things. I'm too scared to drive on highways. I'm not afraid of flying, but I'm scared to death of airports, especially crowded airport waiting areas. So I haven't been able to go with my husband on any of his business trips. I'm afraid to talk to strangers on the phone. . . ."

She shrugged and gave me a rueful smile. "I guess you're probably thinking that I'm afraid of life."

"I'm thinking that fearing all those things must be overwhelming for you," I replied. "I wonder how it would be to take one thing you fear and work on feeling less afraid, little by little, of that one thing."

"I'd be less afraid if it weren't something big, like something my husband is insisting that I get over, like the airport thing, which is so scary for me, too much to handle first thing," she said, twisting a nearly shredded tissue in her hands.

"What would feel most doable at first?"

She smiled. "You're going to think this is crazy," she said. "But I was just thinking that maybe my fear of animals, of cats, might be something we could work on at first. I haven't always feared animals, at least some. I had a hamster when I was in sixth grade. I wasn't afraid of him at all. He was so sweet. I called him Harry. Maybe I could work with your cat if he isn't . . . like . . ." Her hands shook slightly and she looked away.

"If he isn't too big and scary. Is he a big cat? Does he ever bite? Or scratch?"

I reassured Carly that Timmy had never bitten or scratched anyone—in therapy or at home—and that, while he was a large male cat, he was very gentle. I suggested that we start just looking at pictures of him and getting into a pattern of dealing with her anxiety as it came up.

She looked at some pictures and her anxiety rose. I helped her practice deep breathing as a self-calming exercise. Then we explored the thoughts about him that she found scary and she practiced saying "Stop!" when a negative thought came up and substituting a more positive thought, like how good it would feel to pet Timmy and hear him purr.

Finally, a week later, it was time for them to meet. Timmy stood across the room and looked at her. I gave him a hand signal to stay.

"You're in control," I told Carly. "It's up to you to decide whether you want him to get closer. When you want him to get closer, just look in his eyes and say his name."

It took a few minutes of deep breathing before she could look at Timmy directly. Finally, she said his name softly. He walked slowly to her side and looked up at her.

She put a hand down to pet him, then hesitated.

"Think of Harry and how sweet he was," I suggested. "Just touch Timmy's fur very lightly and think of Harry."

She touched him—lightly, tentatively at first, and then started petting him enthusiastically. Encouraged, Timmy stood on his hind legs and put his front paws on Carly's knees, looking into her eyes.

I could feel her anxiety start to rise. "Breathe, Carly," I said softly. "Deep breath in, exhale . . ."

She reached out and stroked his head. "He's so sweet," she said at last. "Who would have thought, I'm not scared—um, as scared—to touch a cat!"

Gradually, over time, Carly tackled her other fears, often with Timmy purring on her lap. She would touch him and remember that she had conquered one fear and other fears could be conquered as well. It wasn't an easy process for Carly. Sometimes we needed to talk about the painful feelings and triggers behind her anxiety.

Carly was the only daughter of parents who were well-known restaurant owners at a popular resort. Her parents were gregarious, outgoing, larger than life. From her early years, her family had teased Carly about her shyness, her reclusiveness, her lack of initiative. "All I've heard all my life is what I lack," she told me. "My two brothers were always right there, learning the business, greeting patrons, going to college, making our parents proud. I was just mousy little Carly.

They told me the only hope I might have in life would be to marry someone who could take care of me. They didn't really think I would ... but I did. And my husband is great. He's really patient with all my fears. If I'm too afraid to go to a social event, he'll stay home with me or go by himself. He doesn't force me into anything. But he would like me to overcome some of my fears, like being afraid to be in airport waiting areas. It's funny, but I'm not afraid of flying. It's just the airport waiting area with all those people. And I'm afraid of driving on highways and freeways with all those cars. And phone calls to strangers, like making a doctor's appointment—oh, my God!"

Some fears were more difficult to tame than others. There were times of triumph and times of backsliding. There was the time when Carly managed to drive from one off-ramp to the next on a busy local freeway without overwhelming anxiety. That was huge and came after many tears, many excursions on surface roads, sometimes having to pull over in a panic. It came after a number of last-minute maneuvers to avoid getting on a freeway. Now encouraged, Carly drove on the freeway past two off-ramps the next week. Soon, she was driving the less trafficked part of their usual route to visit her parents in Big Bear Lake.

The phone calls were harder. She wrote out scripts to make appointments or inquiries. Sometimes she slammed the phone down in a panic when the other person answered. Increasingly, though, she made it through her script. And as we rehearsed in our sessions, she would hold Timmy in her arms, stroking his fur to soothe her anxiety.

Carly's fear of airport waiting areas was more of a challenge. Desensitization exercises meant trips to a local airport with her husband. They chose Hollywood-Burbank, a smaller Los Angeles–area commercial airport, to do their homework. While post–9/11 security measures precluded them practicing in an actual gate waiting area, Carly and her husband found acceptable substitutes in the airport's seats in the ticketing and in the outdoor baggage claim areas. Little by little, she increased her tolerance for crowds, able to stay for ever-lengthening times in these terminal areas teeming with travelers, attendants, and noise. After she had been visiting Hollywood-Burbank Airport for several months without a panic attack, they decided to tackle the big project: leaving for their Hawaiian anniversary trip from the bustling LAX International Airport.

"I did it!" she cried, running into my office, gleeful and tanned, after their return. "Okay, so I wasn't a pretty sight, but I did it!"

She collapsed laughing on the couch and took Timmy into her lap. "So, okay . . . this is what I did. I chewed gum and cried a little and pretended to read a book while I did deep breathing and thought-stopping and meditation exercises. But I did it. And it was so worth it. We had a great time! Wonderful memories. We're both so happy. My husband said he was so proud of me."

Timmy stretched languidly on her lap, and she rubbed his belly. "I'm proud of me, too," she said, addressing Timmy. "And it all started with you, big guy!"

Timmy and Sue:
Rediscovering Passions and Finding Joy

S ue, a thirty-seven-year-old divorced insurance agent with two teenage boys in residence, had been seeing me for a while before she asked for animal-assisted therapy. Her low-level chronic depression kept her from enjoying life, although not from doing what she needed to do on a daily basis.

"It's just that everything seems like such an ordeal," she told me. "It's like trying to run in mud up to your knees. I don't get any pleasure from anything. It's like everything is an obligation, you know?"

Medication had helped a little. So far, therapy had helped—but just a little. Sue said she would like to meet Timmy "because animals always make me smile. And that would help—just to smile."

Timmy was happy to accommodate this need. He pranced into the office from his carrier in the adjacent bathroom, carrying his red ribbon in his mouth like treasured prey.

Sue smiled and greeted him.

But Timmy was elusive with her initially. He was cheerful and in showing-off mode: talking to himself in little chirps and trills as he raced around the room with the ribbon. Then he dropped the ribbon, chased his tail for a minute or two, and recaptured the ribbon for another trot around the office.

"He has so much energy!" Sue said, still smiling.

"Do you remember a time when you felt that happy and energetic, Sue?" I asked.

"Yes," she replied. "It seems like a long time ago. But it wasn't really. It was, like, three years ago when I used to take an adult tap class at the Y. That was so much fun! I loved the dancing and the people were so nice. And . . ."

"Why did you stop?"

"Why?" She looked at me incredulously. "Because I got divorced. Because suddenly I had to do it all for the boys and work full time and be there for them and . . ."

Sue stopped, suddenly exhausted.

"How much time would it take to do this one thing for yourself? An hour or two? Once or twice a week?"

"Once," she said wistfully. "Except I've gained about thirty pounds and I'm embarrassed."

"Do you remember all the people in the class having perfect bodies?"

"No, but . . ." Sue paused and watched Timmy cavorting. "Well, maybe . . . I'll look into it."

I didn't press her on the topic for the next session or two. Timmy continued to be so playful during the times with Sue that he needed a quick nap afterward.

A month later, Sue brought me a brochure with circled classes. "I've signed up for two classes," she said, handing me the brochure. "See? Here . . . adult tap and then tai chi. I heard from a friend that tai chi is very soothing and that it helps your balance. So I decided I am going to do two things just for me."

Timmy suddenly sat down beside Sue and put his head on her lap, resting and purring. She smiled and stroked his head softly.

"And how do you feel about doing a few things just for you?"

"Mostly good. A little guilty. It's time away from my kids, but I'm hopeful that it will be a nice break for all of us and that they're old enough not to burn the house down when I'm away for an hour."

There was a liveliness in Sue's eyes and in her bearing that I hadn't seen before. I told her what I was noticing.

She looked pleased, then glanced down at Timmy. "I'm not yet at the energy level of this one," she said. "But let's just say, well, I'm cautiously optimistic. And any sort of optimism for me is a big step forward!"

Timmy and Irene: Releasing the Burden of Bitterness

When some patients enter the room, there is a mood, an aura, an atmosphere that comes with them. With Irene, it was a miasma of anger, sadness, and an unspoken warning not to get too close.

The straightforward facts about her situation spoke of loss and loneliness: her husband of forty-seven years had died of cancer within the last few months, her forty-three-year-old daughter had withdrawn from her after a series of recent rows, and she felt that she had no friends among her neighbors in the over-fifty-five mobile home park where she and her husband had lived for the past fourteen years.

She didn't know why she had asked for animal-assisted therapy except that she trusted animals more than people—which wasn't saying a lot—and that she was still pretty put out with her medical doctor for referring her to psychotherapy before even thinking of prescribing an antidepressant.

"He said he thought it would be good for me to talk to someone instead of just popping a pill," she said, avoiding my gaze. "But how is talking supposed to make this better? You can't bring my husband back. You can't change my stubborn daughter's mind. So what good is this? I might as well have a few sessions where I can pet a cat. I always wanted a cat, but we could never have one because Jack had asthma and was allergic to furry animals."

I nodded. "Animals can be a great comfort," I said. "I'm glad you asked to work with Timmy. Perhaps if you begin to feel better within, you can find a way to reconcile with your daughter and to heal your understandable grief. And if you want to sign a paper so your doctor and I can confer, we might be able to help you to combine psycho-therapy and drug therapy. How does that sound to you?"

She shrugged. "Give me the paper to sign, and I'll sign," she said at last. "Now, where's the cat?"

I opened the bathroom door and Timmy came out slowly, stretch-ing as he emerged. He stopped and looked at Irene. She looked at him. They were sizing each other up.

"He's not a very attractive cat, is he?" she observed. "Is he hairless? What's the deal with his fur? He has a skinny tail. Why would some-one want to pet him anyway?"

I explained that Timmy was a Burmese–red tabby mix. The very short, cream-colored fur and skinny tail were part of his Burmese heritage. The faint red markings that gave him a peachy, flesh-colored glow were from his red-tabby mother.

"He isn't the most beautiful-looking cat you'll ever meet," I told her. "But he has a wonderful spirit. He is very sweet and loving—and extremely intelligent. His beauty is within."

She looked unconvinced. "He's just a cat," she said.

As if in protest, Timmy began to talk to her in a series of complex mews, trills, and chirps. Then he crossed the room slowly and deliberately, jumped up on the couch, and sat beside her—close enough for her to touch him easily, far enough away to feel safe.

She began to pet him slowly as he watched her closely. "He feels good," she said at last, her shoulders relaxing visibly.

It was the modest beginning of a therapeutic breakthrough for Irene. As the weeks went by, Irene and Timmy snuggled ever closer as she began to talk about the complex feelings that were darkening her days and disturbing her nights. She felt shame that she had spent much of her marriage disliking her husband, thinking about divorce but afraid to step out on her own. When he became ill, she had cared for him but sometimes found herself wishing that he would die months before he actually did.

When Irene's husband died, her grief surprised her. It also shocked her daughter, long accustomed to her mother's unending complaints about the father their daughter had always loved. Grieving and angry over her loss, she accused her mother of being a hypocrite, pretending to have love and feelings of loss that couldn't possibly be real. Then she stormed out of her mother's life, leaving Irene feeling both bereft and guilty.

"I can see how she would feel that way," Irene said quietly, bending over Timmy as she stroked him in an effort to hide her sudden tears.

And as she hugged and stroked Timmy, who snuggled against her, Irene and I talked about the complexity of feelings in many intimate relationships, the impossibility of anyone outside a marriage—even one's child—understanding the true dynamics of a long marriage, the shock and surprise of the intensity of grief, the authenticity of conflicted feelings.

As she came to accept and embrace both her love for and anger with her deceased husband, Irene's protective armor of chilly distance and preemptive judgments began to fade.

She reported having a reasonably relaxed Sunday brunch with her daughter, where they took the first tentative steps toward emotional reconnection. She began to talk with neighbors at her community pool and signed up for a community volunteer project at an area elementary school. The tautness around her mouth eased, and she started to smile more readily.

One day she looked down at Timmy, snoozing on her lap, and smiled.

"You know," she said, stroking under his chin, just the way he liked it most. "Timmy really is a lovely cat in his own way. I mean, outside as well as in. How could you think he isn't beautiful? Look at those sweet little red accent marks above his eyes, like little eyebrows! He is beautiful!"

I smiled. "Yes, you're right, Irene," I said, watching the two of them cuddle in a room that suddenly seemed to glow with light and hope.

Timmy and Richard: The Power of Negativity

Timmy's experience as a therapy cat in my psychotherapy practice wasn't invariably filled with sweetness, light, and hope.

There was one patient Timmy would have nothing to do with. He adamantly refused to engage with him.

His name was Richard.

Richard was an insurance-company referral who came into therapy complaining of depression "because my life is shit."

It didn't take much to convince me that Richard's life, indeed, had its complications. He had been married and divorced three times, with one adolescent or young adult child from each marriage. He had contentious relationships with all three ex-wives and ongoing financial disputes over child support raging with his second and third ex-wives. His eldest son was in prison. His two younger kids were both in and out of rehab for drugs and alcohol. While Richard had a good job, he felt that he didn't have good relationships with his boss or coworkers and feared losing his job "because I just can't kiss ass like most people seem to know how to do automatically." He had enjoyed a close relationship with his never-married sister until he took one of her credit cards without her knowledge and used it to finance a nearly

$3,000 gambling spree. His sister, now estranged, had threatened to call the police and report his theft of her card.

He asked for animal-assisted therapy, "because people don't tend to like me."

Timmy didn't like him either.

Hunkering suspiciously on the other side of the room as Richard told his story, Timmy turned his back to him, curled up, and settled in for a nap.

"Timmy!" I said softly. "Timmy! Come on. Richard needs to talk with you. He wants to pet you."

Timmy looked at me and then looked away, a cranky meow coming from somewhere low in his throat.

"Looks like this guy needs more training to be a therapy cat!" Richard said, smiling. He got up and walked across the room to Timmy, reaching down to pick him up. Suddenly, uncharacteristically, Timmy stood up, his skinny tail instantly fat and quivering. Glaring at Richard, he emitted a lingering, low growl. In almost eight years of knowing and loving Timmy, I had never heard him growl before.

"He's having an off day, obviously," I said, puzzled. "Let's leave him alone and just talk. Maybe he'll come around."

So Richard talked—and the more he talked, the more I felt like growling, too. He refused to take any responsibility for his own life and his own choices. He had no empathy for those close to him. He didn't see anything terribly wrong with gambling on his sister's credit card. "Yeah," he said with a sigh. "So you think I should have asked her first?"

Timmy, muttering to himself, stalked out of the room and into the adjacent bathroom.

I asked Richard if he thought that his gambling, which appeared to be complicating his closest family relationships and preventing him from meeting his financial obligations to his children, might be a major factor in his difficulties.

He angrily dismissed the suggestion. "It's a hobby," he said. "It's my only interest in an otherwise pretty boring life. I don't want to give it up."

I observed that many people hit casinos on a purely recreational basis, deciding in advance how much money they could afford to lose and sticking to that budget, enjoying the casino experience without risking their personal financial stability. But if gambling became something else, if it began to interfere in a number of ways with important relationships, if it caused one to become unable to meet essential financial obligations, then perhaps it was an addiction rather than a hobby. And perhaps a 12-Step program, at the very least, could be helpful.

He shrugged, unconvinced, unwilling to entertain the notion that his hobby was no longer a harmless pastime.

"I thought you'd tell me how to be happier in my life instead of ragging on me," he said sullenly. "Even your cat wasn't nice to me."

At the end of the session, Richard wrote me a twenty-dollar check for his copay. The check bounced. He gave me a credit card number. It was maxed out.

He never returned for another session.

TIMMY'S ENDURING LESSONS FOR PATIENTS—AND FOR ME

In his work with all the patients above—except for Richard —Timmy offered some enduring lessons that resonated with patients and with me:

🐾 **Make self-care a priority.** As giving as he was, Timmy was scrupulous about self-care. If he wanted a snack, he would ask for it. If he needed a nap, he would curl up for a quick snooze. He got plenty of exercise romping and playing—in and outside of therapy sessions. He groomed himself meticulously and always looked splendid.

It wasn't that I could have romped or eaten or snoozed in session. But watching him attend to his needs made me take a look at my own life and how I wasn't making myself a priority.

At my second job at a psychiatric clinic so busy that there were few breaks between patients, I used to lunch on instant Go-Gurt—the yogurt in a tube that you could squirt into your mouth in a second and then go on. I took bathroom breaks only before sessions with established clients with whom I felt comfortable saying, "This will just take a minute," or who might invite me to take time from their session for a little self-care.

During one session I was so exhausted that I actually fell asleep and slipped out of my chair onto the floor in front of a frantic clinic patient who thought that I had fainted.

I did indeed faint in front of another patient during a late-day session on my first day back in the clinic following thoracic surgery. Bowing to pressure from a clinic manager who threatened to transfer my clients to other therapists if I didn't return immediately, I had come back to work after three weeks instead of the four weeks my doctor had ordered.

I was aware of the irony of my urging my patients to take good care of themselves while I kept up this punishing schedule. But it was the experience of watching Timmy give but also take good care of himself that made the most lasting impression. In caring for others, he never neglected himself.

He also taught self-care by valuing others—patients like Linda and Sue, who were caregivers and mothers, as well as Brittney, who was challenged with raising herself to be someone, to reach her goals, with little encouragement from others. Timmy prompted them to care enough about themselves to carve out time and to do good things for themselves because they were worth it. Timmy cuddled and loved them into the habit of self-care.

❧ **Use excitement to bring joy and energy to your life.** It's quite common in therapy to suggest that a mildly depressed client try acting "as if"—as if happy rather than depressed. When a person is able to do this, quite often that person's mood improves. Sometimes the smile comes before the feeling; combined with the positive reactions from others as well as the physical benefits of smiling, laughing, and seeming happy, a person can experience a new feeling of lightness and a lifting of the depressed mood.

There is a scientific basis for this reaction. Numerous studies suggest that facial expressions have more impact on emotions than either thoughts or memories. Researchers have found that facial expressions affect the temperature of blood flowing to the brain, possibly affecting brain areas regulating emotions. This effect holds whether someone smiles naturally or whether subjects had chopsticks holding their mouths into the approximation of a smile. Although theories about the link between facial expressions and subsequent emotions are still somewhat controversial, this phenomenon has been noted for well over a century; Charles Darwin and William James noted that facial expressions, besides showing emotions, may actually contribute to them.

Allowing yourself to look and act happy and excited may lead to genuine excitement as you learn to view your life and the world around you in a new way.

Many patients come in complaining that their lives are boring, with no excitement and no energy to create excitement in their lives. These patients, too, often have an underlying depression and flat expressions, devoid of life. They may have a "I've seen it all, done it all" attitude. And they feel stuck.

Getting unstuck can be a matter of allowing excitement into one's life. As we grow up—in an effort to be cool, sophisticated adults—we tend to extinguish that natural exuberance that we see in young children—and in cats.

My clients and I would watch with wonder at times as Timmy explored all means of play with his red ribbon—leaping, pouncing, rolling around with it, discovering it as if for the first time.

If we can consciously cultivate some of that excitement into our own lives—whether getting excited by a lovely flower or sunset or first sight of the ocean in the summer or seeing a friend or beloved family member, or discovering a new idea or interest—our lives can become richer, fuller, and rarely, if ever, boring.

❖ **Curiosity builds connections.** I thought about curiosity and connecting while watching Timmy get to know patients. He observed them carefully. He approached gently, with interest. He sniffed and walked all around them. He touched. He cuddled. All this time, his attention was focused on this new person.

It made me think about how it is with humans—in the therapy room and socially. As therapists, we ask initial session/intake questions, sometimes determined by a clinic in which we may be working, sometimes dictated by an insurance company or by bureaucratic necessity rather than true curiosity. Socially we may miss chances for real intimacy by sticking to the conventional line of questioning—the accepted form of human sniffing around one another—by asking what a person does for a living, how many children they have, where they're from originally, and so on.

But if we focus on another—whether a new acquaintance or a patient—and ask questions that stem from curiosity and from true interest in that person, the chances for a warm connection vastly improve. Listening rather than planning a response, immersing oneself in the unique life story of another rather than rushing in with advice and reveling in one's own cleverness and insight, can make a huge difference.

I remember once looking on with horror during a therapists' and supervisors' community meeting at my first internship. A fellow intern—whom I knew slightly from graduate school—spoke up about her progress with one of her clients. "Sometimes I'm just blown away by my own brilliance," she said. "I leave the therapy room saying to myself, 'You are so, so, so good!'" And she kissed herself repeatedly on each arm.

I wanted to jump up and scream, "But this isn't about you! It isn't about your supposed brilliance. It's about the patient, for heaven's sake! This is their therapy! Why aren't you focusing on the patient?"

Instead, I took a deep breath and glanced over at the supervisors, waiting for one of them to say something, as meeting protocol required. No one said anything.

Fortunately, this young woman lost interest in being a therapist before completing the required 3,000 hours of internship and so was never licensed.

But I've never forgotten the lesson reinforced then: it's about the patient, not you. And that—as well as the wonderful example that Timmy gave me—helped to keep my focus where it needed to be in therapy—and in life outside the office.

There is such a wonderful difference in a conversation— whether in the therapy room or socially—when you engage with interest, asking leading questions. You have a chance to learn so much more from and about a person, an opportunity to get to know someone in whole new ways.

❖ **Fun and play have a place—even in the most challenging of times.** We can find rest and comfort in levity, even during a time of great pain. Sometimes we forget this and chastise ourselves for smiling, even laughing, when we feel we should be grieving nonstop.

Timmy seemed to know the value of playful distraction as he worked with patients—sometimes cuddling up to comfort them, sometimes seeking to distract them from their pain or anger by inspired silliness and playful antics. He helped many patients take a break from their stress, sadness, or anger and simply enjoy a moment. He gave a vivid demonstration of the fun of being in the moment—the fun of being real—to Peter, the television producer who was feeling that life had lost its zest. He charmed Irene into starting to let go of her bitterness and begin to smile again.

Timmy's talent for bringing levity to challenging times is a variation on laughing between one's pain—fully experiencing moments of pleasure between the painful times—which gives one the strength and perspective to deal with the next wave of pain.

❧ **When in doubt, reach out. Take the risk of reaching out to those who aren't friendly as well as those who obviously like you.** It's so easy to share love with someone who obviously likes you, whether you know that person well or not.

It's a much greater challenge to approach someone who is more distant, if not outwardly hostile.

Although all the patients who worked with the therapy cats were screened and no true cat phobics either volunteered for or were accepted into animal-assisted therapy, some patients who did participate were less enthusiastic than others. I learned a lot from Timmy's interactions with Irene, whose first impression of him was critical, observing that he wasn't a very attractive cat. She regarded him warily as he approached her and then jumped up on the coach beside her. He gave her the space to get to know him gradually, sitting calmly as she petted him, tentatively at first. But he stayed by her and, over time, helped her to open her mind and heart to new ways of loving and seeing the world around her.

I was thinking of Timmy and Irene when I arrived at my fiftieth high school reunion not long ago and the first person I encountered of my forty-three classmates (it was a small Catholic girls' high school) was a woman I had considered so intimidating in her adolescent hostility and disdain that I actively avoided her when we were young. We never spoke to each other, never attempted a conversation, when we were in high school.

Now we were face to face, and I was amazed to see her, knowing that she had traveled a long way from her home and life as an ex-pat in Mexico to be there. Impulsively, I threw my arms around her and told her how happy I was to see her. She smiled with surprise and wonder, then she hugged me enthusiastically. She later told me the story behind her stormy demeanor in high school—the story of a young girl who felt dumped in boarding school as an incomprehensible punishment by her parents, a young girl who was scared and lonely, who felt like an outsider as a non-Catholic in a Catholic school and who thought I was a "religious fanatic brainiac" and so kept me at arm's length with her attitude.

As the evening went on, we dished about our least favorite nun, about the lessons learned through our journeys in life, about how misleading first impressions can be. There, in the glow of a warm reconnection, we rediscovered each other—as friends. Love and warm reconnections prevailed throughout the wonderful two-day reunion, but there wasn't anyone I enjoyed being with more than this woman who had so intimidated me in our youth. She had been a good friend to many, a loving wife and mother, a successful businesswoman throughout the years since we were classmates. But it wasn't until I took the risk of showing joy and affection first that I had a chance to discover for myself the lovely person she really was.

This life lesson was, without a doubt, straight from Timmy.

Four:

TIMMY—
THE INSPIRATION

Not all of the patients whose lives Timmy touched worked directly with him.

Mariana was one of my clinic patients. I supplemented my private-practice income with work at a psychiatric clinic dedicated to helping patients who had life-changing or life-threatening conditions due to at-work injuries. The pace was frantic: I would see perhaps ten to fourteen individual patients a day, as well as running a large support group. Animal-assisted therapy was not and could not have been part of the therapeutic mix.

Timmy, from afar, still touched the life of one of these patients.

Mariana, a Romanian immigrant who had worked on the production line for a small manufacturing company in Burbank that made orthopedic braces and medical devices, had sustained significant back and shoulder injuries due to the repetitive motions required in her eight-hour workday, unrelieved by any breaks, even bathroom breaks. She also had cardiac problems and needed life-saving surgery. Her cardiologist, however, feared that the surgical outcome would not be optimal until she had therapy to deal with her overwhelming depression and anger over her plight. Mariana was not at all pleased with his directive.

She arrived, mute with fury, for her first session with me, accompanied by her young daughter Diana, who had taken time off from her teaching position to bring her mother in and act as interpreter. "She's so mad about coming, she says she won't speak English to you," Diana explained. "So the doctor here said I could be her interpreter."

I nodded. I had several non–English speaking patients—from Vietnam, Thailand, and Sri Lanka—who communicated through medical interpreters.

I had many more patients who had arrived at their initial sessions angry and frustrated at being referred by their physicians for psychotherapy. Many would never have set foot in a therapy office otherwise. Some were upset that critical surgery or physical treatment was being supplemented or even delayed for psychotherapy. For others, anger masked fear.

In other words, angry new patients were quite common—and even though each initial session was fairly tightly structured with certain questions we were required to ask, I was usually able to reassure anxious and angry patients in the course of that first session.

But Mariana was not to be reassured or soothed or otherwise charmed.

Her reaction to my first question was stormy and in English. "Stupid question!" she shouted, standing up to her full 4'10" height and glaring at me. "You're stupid!"

"Mama!" Diana tugged at her sleeve. "Mama! Sit down and listen to the doctor."

Her eyes never leaving mine, the anger firmly etched on her face, Mariana sat down.

Each question I asked elicited the same reaction. After fifty minutes of "You're stupid!" I was exhausted. Stella, the biofeedback technician working in the room next door, peered in just after the pair left. "Well," she said, "if it's any consolation, my guess is that they won't be back."

But they were back the next week, with Mariana looking as angry as ever. When she sat down in the chair in front of me, her ever-vigilant daughter by her side, her glare had lost none of its intensity. I sat wondering what I could ask that would help to break that barrier of anger and resentment.

I heard myself wondering aloud. "I just wonder what matters to you in life, Mariana," I said. "Besides your wonderful daughter, what matters most? What makes you want to get up in the morning?"

The anger faded. Her eyes smiled. "My doggie," she said.

"Tell me about your doggie."

In a rush of enthusiasm, she began to tell me about her Pomeranian mix Nanuk, how beautiful and sweet he was, how close he had been to her Russian Blue cat, Vladimir, until Vlad had licked some medicinal ointment from a wound on Nanuk's foot and died as a result. Her eyes filled with tears. "My fault," she said quietly. "I should have watched more carefully. I blame myself for so much." She wiped her eyes.

"It's so sad when you love an animal or a person so much and yet you can't always protect them," I said. "I get the feeling that you took wonderful care of Vlad. It was just a terrible thing that happened when Vlad was trying to take care of Nanuk."

Mariana wiped her eyes again and nodded, looking at me, suddenly connecting in a new way.

"You understand," she said, brightening a bit. "You like animals? You have a dog? Or a cat?"

"I have two cats," I told her. "They're brothers named Timmy and Gus. They're very sweet and loving. Timmy even works with me, comforting some patients in my private practice. I carry their picture with me." I fished it out of my briefcase and handed it to her.

She smiled and studied the photo. "Oh!" she said. "They're beautiful cats! They love each other like Vlad and Nanuk. You take good care of them, I think."

"Yes," I said as she handed the picture back to me. "I love them a lot, just as you've loved Nanuk and Vlad. Do you have a picture of them?"

Her smile broadened. "I'll bring!" she said. "Next time!"

The next week, she arrived with a photo album of pictures of Nanuk and Vladimir—and with Nanuk in tow. He sniffed me curiously and allowed me to pet him. She was delighted. "He likes you!" she said. "He approves. Diana, it's okay. You can go sit in the waiting room. I'll talk to the doctor here. She's okay. She likes animals, too!"

And so we talked, for months and years, about her feelings, her life, her difficult escape with teenage Diana from Romania just before Christmas in 1986 when that country was still in the grips of a communist dictatorship.

She hadn't left Romania because of the country's political climate. She had grown up with that. Her reasons were much more personal. Her husband, a businessman whose work often took him abroad, had defected to the United States during a business trip several years before, leaving Mariana and Diana in Romania to live with the devastating repercussions. Mariana was taken into custody for weeks-long interrogations at regular intervals as officials grilled her about her husband's whereabouts. Diana, an excellent student, was suddenly denied education and work, confined to their home, and terrified when officials would hammer on the door, calling her names, while her mother was at work.

Mariana was a bright woman whose family circumstances had precluded a college education. Nevertheless, she had advanced well in her work in programming and data entry at a telecommunication center. After her husband's defection, however, she was demoted to telephone operator and moved constantly to different work locations around Bucharest.

But beyond all of the fallout from her husband's defection, Mariana felt strongly that her daughter deserved an intact family and applied to leave Romania and join her husband in the United States. The process took several years—more stress, more interrogations. They were forced to leave most of their money and belongings behind.

However, when the family was reunited in the United States, Mariana realized that the marriage was beyond repair. She and her husband divorced, and she settled into life as a single mother in Los Angeles, supporting the family while Diana excelled academically in high school, college, and later in her work as a teacher. A dedicated worker, Mariana was frustrated over being injured. She feared her health failing just when she needed so much to be there for her ninety-year-old mother, who lived with them now and who had been diagnosed with Alzheimer's. All she wanted for Diana was for her not to have to be a caregiver for her and for her grandmother but to find true love and have a family, a happy life, of her own.

Settling into her therapy with me, Mariana explained her early anger in our sessions. Her culture did not look kindly on psychiatry and psychotherapy; personally, she could not see the use of it. Could talking about her feelings obliterate the horrors of being left behind in Romania to face interrogations that lasted around the clock for weeks? Could it make those times she watched her daughter suffer the consequences of her father's choice any less bitter? Could talking cure her back or shoulder or heart? As much as I might care, could I—or anyone—heal her past?

Despite her perceived limitations of therapy in healing the pain of her past, Mariana began to see the possibilities of the present, relaxing as she talked, even laughing again. And she always asked about

Timmy and Gus, smiling as she looked at their picture—which she asked to see at every session.

When her cardiologist finally scheduled her risky heart surgery, Mariana had one request. "Maybe this is asking too much, but it's my heart's desire," she said one day, watching my face carefully. "I want so much to meet your Timmy and Gus. I want to hold them and kiss them. I know them so well from that picture. I just want to meet them now in case I die and never have another chance."

It was such a heartfelt request. Timmy and his brother had already, from a distance, helped Mariana to feel safe with me in therapy. How could I refuse?

After getting permission from the clinic director, I arranged for Mariana and Diana to come to my private-practice office the next Sunday afternoon. Timmy and Gus were there to greet them. Characteristically, Gus was a little shy—which is why he was never a therapy cat—but Timmy went straight to Mariana, perched on the coffee table in front of her, and reached out a paw to touch her face.

She beamed at him. "You are just like I always thought you would be, Timmy!" she said softly. Gus finally came quietly to her side, eager for a share of attention. Mariana bent down to pet him and tell him how beautiful he was.

But it was Timmy who captured her heart. He stepped onto her lap and into her arms. She held him for a long time.

Mariana wasn't the only patient Timmy inspired from afar.

There were others, less contentious at the outset, who smiled at the picture of Timmy and Gus that I kept on my desk at the clinic and quietly decided, in their own ways, that as an animal-lover I was somehow safe as a talk partner.

Some private-practice clients, while they did not opt for any therapy sessions with Timmy, would smile when they saw his picture on the bulletin board and ask how he was doing.

There was Chloe, my first patient on Saturdays who was allergic to cats but who couldn't come another day. Timmy was always secured in the adjacent bathroom while she was there. But she said she could feel his presence in a positive way. "It's hard to explain," she said, smiling toward the door. "But I feel a different energy in the air when he is there."

I did know what she meant. Timmy brought a unique energy to the room, a special kind of caring and comfort when he was around.

He helped me to relax and be more present with patients. He helped me to stop trying so hard to help—and to simply be with another person.

He helped me to be more patient, more watchful. Seeing Timmy, I was newly aware of the importance of being present in the moment, of listening without planning a response, hearing without rushing in immediately with an intervention. I learned, with new emphasis, the importance of waiting as a patient puzzled or cried or raged through pain and confusion.

Timmy made me increasingly comfortable with silence. Comfort with silence was something I had been working on for years. As a journalist, I had become quite adept at letting silence fall and looking at my interview subject expectantly, maybe with slightly raised eyebrows, waiting for the person to say more. As a therapist I had learned to react to and use silence less obviously, with a softness of expression and a warmth of connection that felt safe to the patient.

I became even more sensitive to approaching each new patient as a distinct individual as I watched Timmy so uniquely relate to each one of the clients with whom we worked together. With a patient who was anxious or defensive, he never rushed to connect. He simply sat at a comfortable distance and let them make the first moves. With patients who were sad, he would sometimes be quick to console them, sometimes seek to distract them—with playful, distracting antics at their feet or inviting them to chase him to capture his treasured red ribbon. With an angry patient, he would sit quietly, ready to soothe.

While he could and did relate to patients in very different ways than I could, it quickly became clear to me that our work together was exquisitely entwined. He could offer the physical affection that I could not give private-practice clients. He could be playful and have fun with them while I kept a professional demeanor. Moreover, the warm relationship that Timmy and I had positively affected the patients. Some began to relax with me and trust me more when they saw that I was a genuine animal lover.

I enjoyed this lovely partnership at the office and also at home. The differences between Timmy at work and Timmy at home were subtle but profound. I could feel his body and spirit relax once he was home and reconnected with his beloved brother, Gus. The two would celebrate with a quick nap together and then dinner—different food because their preferences varied—but with dishes closely together and mutual grooming afterward.

Timmy would greet Bob with unrestrained exuberance the minute he would walk in the door from work. Gone was the watchful, careful, sensitive cat therapist. Timmy became like an excited child as he raced down the hall, knowing Bob's footsteps, and leaping into his arms or onto his shoulders, jumping up to hug his leg or pouncing onto the bed and stretching out to greet Bob with a nose touch and kiss.

He loved to be with Bob as much as possible and to do everything that Bob did—from watching television sports to flossing his teeth—and he was quite willing and able to be an in-home cat therapist when the need arose. Bob especially needed his loving care when an episode of his epilepsy-related depression would hit. Timmy and Gus both were quick to respond. Gus sprawled across Bob's lap or his legs, purring. Timmy wrapped around his neck, nuzzling his face, purring softly.

There were times, too, when I needed his therapeutic touch. I remember lying on the bed, wrapped in a robe and reading the Sunday *New York Times* one Mother's Day, trying to ignore the grief I was feeling. In that sense, it was a Mother's Day like any other: a reminder that, unlike what seemed to be the rest of the world, I didn't have a mother and I would never be a mother. Most days of the year, life felt full and satisfying without children. But Mother's Day and the wishes I would get for a happy one—from sales clerks and bank tellers and neighbors who didn't know me well, wishes that assumed I was a mother like everyone else—would get to me, to that small

grieving spot within that pained me in my always quiet, always reflec-
tive Mother's Day.

What was different about Mother's Day 2007 was that Timmy
crawled across the newspapers and lay down in front of me, his eyes
meeting mine. We simply looked at each other as the minutes ticked
by and I felt my sadness leave me. I felt uniquely loved and connected
to this little creature with so much life, so much feeling in his direct
gaze.

"I love you so much, Timmy," I said softly, stroking his face and
listening for his rich purr. "Please live a long time. I can't imagine life
without you."

He looked at me—gently, sweetly, purring—and placed a paw in
my outstretched hand.

It was an incident so sweet, so common, so ordinary in our lives
that it shouldn't stand out so in my memory.

But it does—because by the next weekend, Timmy would
be gone.

Timmy and Gus

Timmy

Five:

THE UNTHINKABLE

At some rare and terrible times in our lives, a newspaper item becomes a headline, and a headline becomes not something just to frown over before turning the page but a life-changing personal tragedy.

The first stirrings of pending disaster had come quietly in the spring of 2007 with some disturbing news items about tainted pet food. The articles were small at first, hidden deep in the news section: items about some common brands of cat foods, including some sold under medical prescription, being tainted by a cost-cutting alternative to wheat products in a Chinese additive that was surprisingly common in American pet foods. Instead of wheat, Chinese manufacturers had substituted ground melamine, a plastic material most commonly seen in unbreakable dishes.

The story crept to the front pages and into the headlines as dozens, then hundreds, then thousands of cats and dogs across the United States began to develop kidney failure. Many died. Alarm spread to the point that newspapers and television news began to direct concerned pet lovers to a website—*fda.gov.org*—to track which foods had been found to contain the potentially lethal additive.

I was among them, logging into the website several times a day. Many familiar brands appeared, but not the foods that either Timmy or Gus favored. Still, I was watchful. I scanned sites about making your own pet food. I went to a pet supply store and sought out grain-free products. Timmy and Gus had long eaten different brands of cat food, Timmy preferring dry food and treats with a little of a favorite wet food. Gus favored wet food only. But both agreed on the new natural, no-grain products: they refused to eat them. After a three-day standoff I went back to giving them the foods they preferred, checking the Food and Drug Administration site daily. Still, their brands of pet food did not appear. I was cautiously optimistic.

Not everyone shared my concerns. Bob and I had dinner with a business friend of his whose wife, a reluctant dog owner because their kids had wanted a puppy, sipped a glass of wine and rolled her eyes when I asked her if she was checking the FDA site. "My husband is into that," she said with a sigh. "Me? I don't worry. Like, our dog's brand of food did appear on the site, along with serial numbers that matched the last case of dog food we bought. It's a whole case! You know how expensive that is? So we're supposed to throw it out? She has eaten three cans and hasn't died yet. So we'll give her the rest and hope for the best. Frankly, I think it's a bunch of hype."

I shuddered at her willingness to take risks with her dog's life. These people lived in a million-plus-dollar mansion. They could certainly afford to throw out the food. But they didn't. And they got lucky. Their dog survived.

We felt lucky though vigilant. Both Timmy and Gus seemed healthy. In fact, Timmy seemed to be putting on a bit of weight. We talked about cutting back his portions and eliminating treats.

Then, the Tuesday after Mother's Day in 2007, we got home from work to find that one of the cats had thrown up in three places. It wasn't a particularly rare occurrence. One or the other would throw up once every few months, particularly Timmy, if he gobbled his food too fast. I checked the FDA website. Nothing new. I watched both cats closely all evening. They both seemed fine.

When I got home from seeing patients late Wednesday evening, Bob greeted me with concern. "When I got home, there was cat vomit in five places throughout the house," he said. "I gave them some dinner, and Timmy threw it up almost immediately. Gus seems fine, but I'm worried about Timmy."

Just then, we heard a sound we had never heard from a cat before: it was a piercing scream followed by retching. We rushed to Timmy's side. He looked at us, trembling. Bob cuddled him in his arms while I called an emergency animal hospital that had just opened nearby.

We rushed him in. The vet there seemed mystified. "His vital signs are fine," she said. "The only thing I can find wrong is that he is a little dehydrated." She suggested giving him plenty of water and taking him to his regular vet in the morning.

When we got home, I sat at the computer, Timmy on my lap, checking the FDA website, doing searches on the food that Timmy had consumed and looking up vomiting as a symptom. His food brand was still considered one of the safe ones. There could be many reasons for vomiting, but none seemed to quite fit. Timmy lay on my lap, watchful and trusting.

His nausea seemed to have passed, but he wanted to stay close. Instead of curling up with Gus in the little bed they chose to share, Timmy insisted on sleeping with us, cuddling up for comfort, purring and rubbing his face against ours.

I met Dr. Tracy as she arrived at her office at 7 AM on Thursday. She frowned as she cradled Timmy in her arms. She said that she would run some tests and that it might be a virus. Once his heart defect had healed when he was still a kitten, Timmy had never been ill in his nearly nine years of life. She suggested that I leave him with her and pick him up that evening after work.

Two hours later, Dr. Tracy called me at my UCLA Medical Center office, where I was now working days, having left the psychiatric clinic. "I can't believe it," she said, her voice choked. "He is in total kidney failure. Has he been in your garage? Could he have ingested antifreeze?"

"No, he hasn't," I whispered, sitting down, shocked.

"He has a urinary blockage, and I don't have the diagnostic equipment here to find out what's causing it," she said. "This is urgent. Could you come get him and take him to VCA West Los Angeles Animal Hospital? I know Dr. Sean Yoshimoto there, and he is excellent. They have all the equipment to diagnose Timmy properly. Can you leave work now, immediately, and come get him? I've already called and made an appointment for Timmy with Dr. Yoshimoto."

The hospital was three blocks from my UCLA office, but thirty-five miles from Timmy. I called Bob at his office in downtown Los Angeles, and we both raced for our cars, getting to Dr. Tracy's at the same time. We bundled Timmy into his carrier, and Bob drove frantically through heavy traffic to get to the hospital.

VCA West Los Angeles was busy and crowded, and the receptionist was brusque. But Dr. Yoshimoto was kind, smiling and cradling Timmy, remarking on how beautiful and well-behaved he was. He said he would need to keep him overnight for tests.

His call on Friday morning brought bad news: Timmy's kidney failure was complete. His urinary blockage—of mysterious origin—was immobile.

"There is the possibility of dialysis," Dr. Yoshimoto said, a bit hesitantly. Grasping at hope, I asked about it, crestfallen to find that the monthly cost for the required lifelong dialysis would be considerably beyond our reach—four times our combined monthly income—and that Timmy could never leave the hospital. He could never come home, never again lead the semblance of a normal life.

"That really wouldn't be possible for us," I said at last.

There was a pause.

"We're going to try one more thing," Dr. Yoshimoto said. "But if that doesn't work, we will need to put him down."

Put him down? My mind raced. But he was fine just a few days ago! But he is my therapy cat! But he is our love.

The phone rang again. It was Mariana, who had survived her risky heart surgery, and who had become, in the years after her clinic therapy ended, an unlikely but treasured friend. I had called her the night before to tell her how worried we were about Timmy. She was calling for an update.

When I told her that the doctor was recommending euthanasia if the last-ditch procedure didn't work, she gasped. "Oh, no!" she said quietly, her voice breaking. "Can't something be done? Remember when Nanuk was attacked by a Rottweiler and his regular vet said he couldn't possibly live? We took him to VCA West Los Angeles. Maybe if you took him there—"

"Mariana," I said, fighting tears. "He is at VCA West Los Angeles."

There was silence for a moment. "Oh, Kathy," she said at last. "How can I help? What can I do to help you?"

There was nothing to be done.

Dr. Yoshimoto called again an hour later to say that they—and Timmy—had run out of options. He told us that Timmy was in agony and that all efforts to flush his system had failed. "We've got him on morphine," he said. "But he is very precarious. A natural death would be horrendous. Euthanasia is the only compassionate option."

If he had to die, couldn't we take him home and have Dr. Tracy, who offered at-home euthanasia, be the one to put him down? Couldn't he leave this life in our arms, in a familiar setting, with his beloved brother, Gus, nearby?

"It's too late for that," Dr. Yoshimoto said quietly. "We need to do it here—and soon. How quickly can you get here?"

As I arranged to leave work early, my coworkers looked on with shock and sympathy. Even my boss, who detested cats in general, embraced me and said she was sorry. Bob picked me up, and we drove to the pet hospital quietly and with a surreal sense that what was about to happen couldn't possibly be happening.

The receptionist was a little less brusque as she directed us to the euthanasia room.

The euthanasia room looked like a small waiting room. There were no examining tables or medical supplies, just a couch, soft lighting, and pictures of clouds and ferns and rainbows on the walls. We were numb with shock as we sat silently waiting.

A technician brought Timmy in, wrapped in a blanket like a baby. He peeked out, and his eyes brightened. She put him on the couch between us, and I was astounded, irrationally reassured, at how well he looked. There must be some mistake. Timmy wasn't dying. He looked as bright and joyous as ever. He rubbed and purred, happy to see us, then seemed puzzled that we weren't swooping him up into his carrier to go home. He got down off the couch, dragging a port attached to his left hind leg behind him. He went to the door, tapped it, and looked at us expectantly.

I felt like scooping him up and running with him from this place, hoping against hope that the doctor was wrong. But I knew he wasn't.

As if from a distance, I could hear Bob talking to Timmy: "Come cuddle with us, Sweetheart. We love you so much."

Timmy began to wander back to us, sniffing the floor and the legs of the couch, and then suddenly he stopped. His whole demeanor changed in an instant. His tail was fat, his fur standing up all over his quivering body. Hyperventilating, crying, he ran around the room, knocking up against walls, throwing himself against the door. He looked at us wildly, fiercely, not hearing our words of love. We tried to comfort him, to pick him up. He would have nothing to do with us.

"I can't stand another minute of this," Bob said at last, so low I could barely hear him. "I'm going out to get the doctor."

As the door closed behind him, I turned to Timmy. "Please, Timmy," I begged. "Please let me hold you and comfort you." I reached out. He edged away, terror in his eyes.

As an anguished memory, across the years to that first day I met Timmy, there was Dr. Tracy's voice: "That little one has fought so hard to live."

Timmy was still fighting hard to live.

When Dr. Yoshimoto entered the room, Timmy's fear seemed to diminish. His face brightened. He stopped shaking. The doctor sat down on the floor, hiding the hypodermic needle under a file he was carrying. Timmy trotted over to him and raised his chin, asking the doctor to scratch his throat. With a smile, the doctor did, petting and calming him.

Bob slipped down to the floor to sit opposite the vet. He reached out his hand to Timmy. Timmy looked in his eyes, frightened, questioning. Then the doctor put the file down and Timmy saw the needle. He drew back, hissing at Dr. Yoshimoto, and struggled to get free of him. The vet put down the needle and cuddled him, rubbing him under the chin.

Then Dr. Yoshimoto began to put the needle into the port on Timmy's leg. Timmy jerked away, dislodging the needle, and, hyperventilating, struggled to get free of Dr. Yoshimoto's arms.

I was trying not to cry, trying not to further alarm him. "Timmy," I gasped. "We love you so much. Timmy—"

He didn't, couldn't hear me. Once again, with Timmy struggling in his arms with a strength born of terror, Dr. Yoshimoto was trying to reattach the needle.

I could see a bead of sweat on the vet's face. "We need—" he said.

Bob looked at Timmy. Their eyes locked. "Timmy, my love, my sweetheart," he said. "Come sit on my lap."

Timmy looked at Bob and his eyes softened. He looked at me. There was love and recognition and a sense of quiet and final resignation.

I slipped down off the couch to sit beside Bob as Timmy gave a little sigh, and, his gaze fixed on Bob, he stepped into his arms.

Dr. Yoshimoto attached the needle to the port and put the blanket on the floor. "Why don't you put him here and keep stroking him and talking to him?" he said gently.

Bob didn't want to let go. But he finally lay Timmy on the blanket, and we both petted him, telling him how much he was loved, how much he would always be loved, how he would live forever and ever in our hearts.

Dr. Yoshimoto leaned over him and put a stethoscope on his suddenly still little body.

There was a moment, and then he looked up at us with a combination of weariness and compassion.

"He's gone."

Timmy and Bob

Six:

WITHOUT TIMMY

week after Timmy's death, his brand of cat food finally appeared on the FDA website's tainted list.

The necropsy report confirmed that melamine had caused his urinary blockage, and that his entire urinary track was filled with melamine crystals. We also had confirmation of our long-held suspicion that our sweet Timmy had, indeed, been short-changed physically all his life. His necropsy revealed that he had only one kidney, explaining, at least in part, the quick and relentless course of his illness.

More newspaper headlines appeared about the ongoing melamine scandal. The Chinese food manufacturer who had deliberately substituted melamine for wheat products in supplements added to U.S.

pet foods had also added melamine to baby formulas in China, to keep costs down and to falsify protein levels in standards testing. When Chinese babies started dying, officials finally started asking questions. When they discovered the deliberate use of melamine in baby formula, justice was swift. The man with ultimate responsibility for melamine-tainted baby formula and pet food was executed immediately.

All of this knowledge and the swift, violent Chinese justice were faint comfort. None of this would bring our one-of-a-kind cat back. Nothing would erase the searing memories of his last days—that piercing scream, the look of terror in his eyes, his desperate fight to live.

I called Dr. Tracy to let her know that Timmy had died. "Oh!" she gasped, as if punched. Her grief took her back years, back to that loving little kitten who had fought so hard to live and a name she hadn't uttered since those days. There were tears in her voice as she said, "Oh, my poor little Blondie."

Patients were stunned. While only two patients—Peter and Irene—were working with Timmy at the time of his death, his passing affected many more.

After Irene pinned a rose next to Timmy's picture on the office bulletin board, patients began to ask questions. News of Timmy's death not only brought sadness and shock but also resurrected major losses in a number of patients: loss of parents, loss of their own beloved pets, the loss of a brother to AIDS, the loss of a child to cancer. We mirrored each other's thoughts and experiences in our grief.

There were tears—for the loss of Timmy and for all the losses the patients had experienced. Old pain of the losses of long-dead beloved pets began to surface in Timmy's patients and in others as well. Lost marriages, lost parents, lost siblings, miscarriages, lost children . . . an outpouring of loss and grief prevailed.

For Peter and Irene, the loss was more immediate and personal.

Peter cried when I gave him the news, telling me, with a touch of amazement, that losing Timmy was nearly as painful for him as losing his beloved dog Alex had been. "I mean," he said, reaching for another tissue and wiping his eyes, "he has been there for me so much over the past two years. Remember when I was so depressed last year that I had trouble talking to you and telling you what was going on? And then Timmy got on my lap and started purring. He was my little buddy. I really got attached. I never thought I would with a cat. But he was so great. I can't believe he's gone." He began to sob.

"He was pure love," Irene said, tears running down her cheeks. "Why? Why? Why? Why Timmy? I'm so angry! It's not right! It's not fair!"

Irene was not alone in her anger. A lot of us were voicing the same ruminations.

The patients and I explored together, in a variety of scenarios, the ways that life isn't fair and how one deals with life's unfairness.

Through it all, I sometimes fought tears as clients cried, and I found myself creating emotional distance from my own sadness.

Though patients knew I had suffered a terrible loss with Timmy's death, we concentrated on their feelings more. I might tell them that I was very sad to lose Timmy, that he was very special to me, and that it was a pain that would take a long time to heal. But I struggled not to cry, not to share my own pain fully.

Although we all talked about the stages of grief and how it was never a straight line from initial shock and denial to acceptance—that a person would make two steps forward and one step back, that progress through pain was often slow and highly individual—I struggled not to let patients see the extent of my devastation. It helped to know that this loss was something we all shared to a certain extent, but I didn't want the focus off my clients and their issues. I didn't want them to feel that they needed to take care of me.

I was a little more candid with former patients who had known Timmy. When Carly, who had moved to another part of the state, phoned to give me an update of her continuing progress against her phobias and anxiety, she asked about Timmy, and I gave her the news. "Oh, no," she cried. But there was no hyperventilating. No anxiety. We both realized it at the same time.

"I'm just sad," she said, with both wonder and grief. "Just so sad. I really loved that little guy. And you . . . how are you doing with this? It must be so hard. I feel so bad for you."

Mariana and Diana came to visit with flowers and hugs. "Kathy," Mariana said softly. "Let me take care of you right now. I'm not your patient anymore, not for three years already. You don't have to worry about me like a patient. Let me worry about you. Let me comfort you."

She rummaged in her bag and produced sandwiches and Eastern European pastries. As Diana arranged the spread on the coffee table, Mariana outlined the agenda. "We'll have a picnic here and eat and cry and talk about Timmy," she said. "And hugs whenever you need . . ."

Despite my sadness, I had to smile. This was so typical of Mariana's loving, generous, maternal, larger-than-life persona. It masked her tiny stature, her frailty, and the fact that, in exactly a year, Mariana would also die.

"Thank you so much," I said, smiling through tears as I embraced her.

The grief at home felt overwhelming at times. While Timmy's loss had a definite impact on my practice, I struggled to keep the focus on patients' feelings and minimize my own. Bob compartmentalized his grief more typically: he said little if anything to coworkers and customers about his feelings of loss, but collapsed in grief when he came home. So did I.

There were times when I tortured myself with "if only's": if only I had insisted on Timmy eating the natural cat food instead of what he preferred; if only I had noticed signs of his illness earlier—like the weight gain due to water retention that may have been an earlier sign of kidney malfunction; if only . . .

And there were times of sudden anger: at the reports of corporate cost-cutting at the heart of the pet food scandal that had cost us our priceless companion and Timmy his life; at the clueless wife of my husband's business companion who knew the batch of dog food she had purchased was tainted, but who fed it to her dog anyway because she didn't want to go to the trouble and expense of throwing it out and buying new food. And, despite it all, her undervalued animal had lived. "Well," she said, languidly drinking yet another glass of wine, "I guess it all has to do with luck, doesn't it? And besides, maybe Timmy didn't die from the cat food. Maybe there was another reason. Or else you guys are just real unlucky."

I willed myself not to throw my water glass in her direction.

At times Bob and I talked about the shock of it all: how in only forty-eight hours Timmy showed the first signs of illness and then, so quickly, he was gone. We grieved at a death that felt so premature. We had cried about losing our seventeen-year-old Freddie. But he had lived a full and happy cat's life. We felt we had done everything we could for him at the end, and that when he did die, it was time. He was old and tired and in pain. Even though we missed him terribly, we found comfort in his life well-lived. With Timmy, there was no such comfort. He had been taken well before his time due to something that didn't have to happen. We missed him desperately.

Timmy's loss left a chasm. Gus, who had been as attached to me as Timmy had been to Bob over the years and who was a much less exuberant cat than Timmy, quite visibly expanded his focus to include cuddling with Bob as he sensed Bob's sadness, but there were gaps even Gus could not fill. The excited greetings. The tussles over dental floss. Timmy wrapped around Bob's shoulders as Bob walked around the house.

I missed my therapy cat—and I missed my unique little companion: his warmth, his energy, his constant stream of conversation in the form of mews, chirps, and trills. We used to joke about "noise pollution" when Timmy was around. But the house now felt so terribly silent . . . except at night.

The nights were when the full extent of Gus' grief was evident. Perhaps he was picking up on our grief. Perhaps he was realizing, as time went on, that his beloved brother was never coming home. Perhaps he was feeling that, without his brother, he was newly alone in the world. It became a sad and unsettling routine. Gus would curl up in the bed he had once shared with Timmy and howl—hour after hour, night after night. We would rush to him and try to comfort him. We would hold him. We would take him into our bed. But he still whimpered and cried and struggled to return to his own bed—and another round of howling.

After some weeks of sleepless nights for all three of us, we went to see Dr. Tracy. When a series of lab tests proved negative for any illness or kidney disorder, Dr. Tracy embraced Gus and buried her face in his fur for a moment. "This poor guy is grieving," she said at last. "He and Timmy were so bonded. All of his life, he has taken care of Timmy. He's not only missing his brother but also his mission in life. Get him a little kitten to nurture."

We took a deep breath. Another kitten? It seemed so soon. Yet Gus was in obvious distress—and our sleep deprivation was a definite problem.

"Maybe we could find another Burmese-mix kitten who would be smart and have a fun personality," I said as we drove home. "It wouldn't be Timmy. But maybe a cat with some of the same genetics would be good for Gus—and for us, too."

Bob shrugged. "I can't imagine another cat. Timmy and Gus were such a great duo. If it weren't for Gus crying all night . . ."

I nodded. "I'll just do an online search in rescue groups and see what comes up," I said without much enthusiasm.

What came up was a notice—sans picture—of a Burmese-mix kitten from a rescue group that had animals available for adoption at a pet store across the street from my UCLA office. I strolled over at lunchtime for a look.

"This one?" the attendant wrinkled her nose and pointed at a scruffy, wide-eyed black kitten, clinging to the bars of her cage and mewing for attention. "She's so ugly that she was dumped into rescue by a Beverly Hills breeder of Bombay cats. Do you know about Bombays? They're hybrids, a mix between sable Burmese and black American shorthairs. They're bred to be beautiful, to look like miniature panthers."

She glanced ruefully in the direction of the mewing kitten. "That one is very sweet," she said. "But she's impossibly scruffy. I'm afraid she'll never be much to look at."

I had to agree that she wasn't a beautiful kitten. She wasn't even cute. But when the attendant took her out of the cage and placed her in my arms, she snuggled and purred.

I took out my cell phone and called Bob, asking him to stop by and take a look at this kitten—who had no name, just a serial number—on his way home from work.

Later, Bob smiled as he looked into her huge, earnest golden eyes. "Sweet and loving is what Gus needs," he said, stroking her rumpled fur.

He looked over at me, grinning at a sudden memory. "Remember twenty-five years ago when we were first looking at the animal shelter for a cat, when we found Freddie?" he asked me. "We originally wanted to get a female cat and name her Maggie? Well, here she is. Here's our Maggie."

He cuddled the purring kitten and scratched under her chin. She looked up at him with contented, half-closed eyes. He smiled again and whispered, "We've waited a long time for you, sweet Maggie!"

Gus embraced Maggie immediately. He dropped to the floor, rolled over onto his back, and let her walk and sniff all over him. He lay still, purring, as she pounced him and nipped him on the throat. Then he got up and started to groom her. The next time I looked over at them, they were in his bed, curled up together for a first nap. The night howling stopped.

I marveled at Gus' resilience. Maggie was his new baby, and he was totally devoted. She followed him everywhere, and he never let her out of his sight. He groomed her, let her eat first, embraced her both waking and sleeping. He was playing again, purring again. He seemed to have let go of the past and welcomed his future with Maggie.

I lagged behind in the letting-go process but made slow steps toward living with sadness while going on with life.

I took Timmy's picture off the office bulletin board and told prospective patients that I was no longer offering animal-assisted therapy. I couldn't imagine I would again. Maggie was wonderful with us, but she had a marked stranger phobia. The doorbell, a stranger, even a friend she had seen before would send her running full-speed into our bedroom and sliding under the bed. She was smart and funny and wonderfully sweet, but Maggie would never be a therapy cat.

There were times when I missed Timmy anew—when I was working with a highly anxious patient who could have benefitted from Timmy's calming presence or when I encountered something that would be a sudden, stark reminder of what was no more. The day I found

Timmy's red ribbon curled behind the file cabinet in my office. The time I picked up Gus for a cuddle and suddenly remembered how wonderful it had felt to embrace both Timmy and Gus together. The times new messages of sympathy reminded me of the enormity of this loss.

One day I opened an email from Julia, Timmy's first client. It had been some years since she had completed therapy, married, had children, and moved to another state. She had kept in touch once or twice a year with cheerful updates that were always a delight.

As I opened her most recent message, I vaguely remembered sending her a short email that Timmy had passed away.

Her reply was simple and heartfelt. "It's so hard to type through my tears," she wrote. "But I want you to know that Timmy will be in my heart always. I will never, never forget him."

Her comforting words stayed with me as I walked into the house after work. We would all miss Timmy forever—and remember him with love and gratitude for all that he gave us in the nearly nine years he was with us.

I passed the bedroom and saw Gus cuddling Maggie as they snuggled between the decorative pillows on our bed. He had just finished grooming her and was looking at her with love and devotion. She looked up at me. That's when I noticed something different.

Was it the result of all the tender loving care from Gus? Or was it because we were falling unmistakably in love with this charming little kitten? But one fact was clear:

Maggie was no longer a scruffy, ugly little kitten.

Suddenly, somehow, she was beautiful.

Seven:

LIVING WITH LOSS AND A TOUGH DECISION

Even though it was notable for the loss of Timmy, 2007 was the last mostly normal year of my private practice.

In 2008, our preparations for retirement began—with a tough decision and an ongoing sense of loss as well as anticipation.

Retirement itself was a longtime goal for Bob and me. He planned to retire from work entirely and devote himself to what pleased him most—music, physical fitness, and continued learning in a variety of topics from history to philosophy, from music theory to quantum physics. My dream was to step away from the whirlwind of multiple jobs—the combination of one full-time and two part-time jobs—I had held in various combinations for many years, and settle into a pleasurable work-and-play routine—doing only the work I enjoyed most and spending my new free time getting healthy and fit.

Our retirement target date was April 2010. I would be sixty-five that month and eligible for Medicare as well as for the minimum pension from UCLA. Bob would turn sixty-six that same month.

While the nature of our retirements and the time line seemed clear by mid-2008, one decision remained: Would we retire in place—staying in our small Valencia, California, home of twenty-nine years? Or would we make another longtime dream reality and move to a larger, newer home? To do that, we knew we would have to leave California, as even our tiny home, if we wanted to buy it today, would be out of our price range. It wasn't just square footage that concerned us in retirement but lifestyle and quality of life.

We loved where we were living. Valencia is a beautiful community thirty miles north of Los Angeles. In our twenty-nine years there, we had seen it grow from a sleepy, rural suburb to a self-contained city of its own with a lively arts presence and all the shopping, restaurants, and entertainment venues we could ever imagine.

But despite growing up in and spending our working lives in Los Angeles, we were open to change, open to the idea of moving to another state for a new start in retirement. Arizona—with its larger, inexpensive homes; wealth of fitness-oriented, active adult communities; tamer traffic; and clearer skies—was beginning to look increasingly attractive. Why not? We no longer had family living nearby. Our parents had died, and our siblings all lived out of state. The reasons to leave California were beginning to exceed our reasons to stay.

This dream of a new life came at a cost: selling a house that had become a beloved home for nearly three decades; leaving behind a number of treasured California friends whom we would not be seeing as often; and, for me, closing my private practice and retiring from my career as a psychotherapist.

It was no small thing. I loved being a therapist and cared deeply about my clients. A private practice takes a lot of time, sacrifice, and hard work to build. A move to Arizona would mean leaving my practice behind, closing that chapter of my life, saying, "Good-bye," to my patients.

Even though writing has always been, in my heart and in reality, my first career, the prospect of retiring from my psychotherapy practice prompted a wave of anticipatory grief. It's very hard to say good-bye and to let go of a much-loved and hard-won career. Yet, as a therapist, you're always saying good-bye.

Clients come and go. Some come for only a few insurance-approved sessions. Some, for a variety of reasons, storm out or leave quietly after one or two therapy sessions. One woman only made it through ten minutes of her first session when she spotted Timmy's picture on my bulletin board and asked if that was my cat. I replied that he was and that he was a therapy cat for a limited number of clients. She rose immediately, shouting, "I can't stand cat people!" and ran from the room, never to return.

Other patients stay and work hard in therapy to explore and resolve the issues behind their depression or anxiety or relationship problems in a process that may last for months or even years. With these longtime clients, good-byes are sometimes poignant yet joyous—like Julia's touching and loving good-bye when she expressed the hope that I would take good care of myself as I had taken of her in our six years of working together in therapy.

Now there were other longtime clients to whom I would be saying good-bye, including Chloe, a young widow who had started seeing me three weeks after her husband had died of a heart attack, leaving her and their infant son. In the nearly ten years I had worked with her, Chloe had gone from depression and despair so deep she was, for a time, unable to care for herself or her baby to a life of healing, joy, and new beginnings. She was a devoted mother and, after eight years, had met and married a wonderful, caring second husband. While she still had some challenges in her life and suffered an occasional panic attack, Chloe was doing well. It would be hard to say good-bye, but perhaps it was time.

Closing a private practice is, ideally, a gradual process, taking place in stages: first, you stop accepting new patients and let your practice shrink by attrition. Then you begin to refer patients to other therapists. In my case, I chose to refer most remaining patients to other therapists, retaining only a small roster of longtime clients, including Chloe, whom I would see in my home office for the last year of my practice. Each stage of this letting-go process was painful, with so much loss, so many good-byes.

At last, it was time to make the first physical move of our long transition process.

One Sunday, Bob and our young friend Ryan Grady arrived to help me move my practice out of the professional medical building and to my home office. Ryan, whom we had first encountered when he was a smart, quirky nine-year-old after he and Bob were matched in the Big Brothers program, had watched with great interest during my transformation from journalist to psychotherapist. Somewhere along the way, he had decided to follow the latter career path as well. Now a young man in his twenties, he was about to start graduate school and his own journey toward becoming a psychotherapist, winding up as I was winding down. I gave him my office couch and many psychology books from my office library. Knowing that some of the staples of my professional life were going to be helping him in his life and work made it a little easier to let go of them. My ending was his new beginning.

It wasn't over yet, of course. I still had ten to twelve months to practice. I still had a roster of longtime clients. But the end was in sight.

I paused at the doorway of my now empty private-practice office. I thought of all the tears and anguish, all the laughter and growth that had taken place over the years within these walls. And I thought of Timmy: how he had filled this room with his presence, dashing around with his treasured red ribbon, sitting quietly in the doorway from the bathroom, sizing up a new client, allowing the client to do the same with him before moving closer, comforting, touching, soothing, purring. I felt that, in yet another way, I was losing him again.

My eyes filled with tears as I turned off the lights for the last time, locked the office door, and then slid the keys under the building management's door.

I had no idea, at that moment, of the joys and challenges to come in a practice that was still vibrant, still active. I had no idea of the tears and laughter, the healing and growth to come with the patients who remained. I couldn't have imagined that, within my home office, there would be another miracle—another therapy cat who would soothe, purr, cuddle, cavort, and comfort in ways both familiar and unique.

Timmy

Eight:

I WASN'T LOOKING FOR A CAT—PART 2

mid our hopes and uncertainties for the future, there was a reassuring constant: Gus and Maggie were a wonderful duo.

Their relationship was different from the one Gus had had with his brother Timmy. He not only took care of her—grooming her, encouraging her to eat her fill before he began to eat his meal, cuddling up with her for naps—but he was also protective of her, catching her in an embrace when we walked in and surprised him or when strangers came to the house. It was as if Gus were telling everyone—including us—"You're not taking *this* companion away from me."

As she grew, Maggie began to reciprocate Gus' tender loving care—grooming him, sharing a treat, letting him win an occasional chase even though she was faster.

Maggie's relationship with Bob evolved wonderfully, too. She sat on his lap for hours. She loved to hop on his shoulder to cuddle and to smooth and groom his hair. Standing on his lap, she would comb through his beard with her claws and then groom that, too.

Maggie, like all the cats before her, was quickly responsive to Bob's mood swings, cuddling up to him when he was depressed and ready for play when the depression lifted.

She has been incredibly active and playful, even into adulthood. Maggie was the first cat we ever had who took fetching seriously. She would pursue and retrieve any object—a stuffed toy, a foil ball, or wadded-up piece of paper—and bring it back, dropping it at our feet and waiting, eager for another pursuit.

She was—and is—unusually smart. While she likes to chase the laser mouse, she quickly figured out its origin. Now, when either of us isn't moving the mouse at the pace she prefers, she'll stop and throw an impatient look in the direction of the hand holding the laser.

Like Timmy, she has her share of obsessions. Perhaps her most fervent ongoing obsession is for foam earplugs that I've often worn to block out the sound of Bob's snoring. We don't permit her to play with these because of the choking hazard, but she craves them nonetheless and tries to pluck them out of my ears while I'm sleeping and spirit them away. She also knows where they're kept—and where they've been kept in the past. When we lived in California and had less drawer space in the bathroom, I kept my stash of earplugs in the sock drawer of my bedroom chest. In Arizona I keep them in a certain bathroom drawer. But whenever I open either drawer—only those two—Maggie instantly materializes, rooting around in the drawer for an earplug.

Bob has developed a very special love for this smart, loving cat who, at seven, is now in early middle age. All he has to do is say her name and she stops instantly, wherever she is, whatever she is doing, and runs to him, sitting at his feet, looking up adoringly. If he asks her to come sit on his lap, she jumps up right away—but she always waits for a specific invitation. It's a relationship unique to them. She is sweet to me and to visitors she knows well, shy with those who are new to her. Bob is, quite obviously, her favorite person, while Gus turned his attention, once more, to me as his primary person.

It was a balance that seemed just right. While we still missed Timmy terribly, our day-to-day life with Maggie and Gus was easy, pleasant, and filled with love and affection. We marveled at how easily, how seamlessly, she seemed to fit in—soothing some of the pain of loss for Bob and much of it for Gus, bringing warmth and laughter where it was so needed and appreciated.

Our family—pets and people—felt wonderfully complete.

One evening in the late summer of 2008, not long after we had returned from our exploratory trip to Arizona and had tentatively made plans to move there two years hence, Bob and I were finishing our weekly grocery shopping when I decided to stop at the store next door—a PetSmart—to see if they had any kitty grass in stock. Bob, exhausted from a long day of work and his grueling commute from downtown Los Angeles, decided to stay in the car and rest while I dashed in to get the kitty grass.

I hurried in and scanned the area by the checkout counters where kitty grass was often displayed. Nothing. I remembered that it was sometimes shelved in another area of the store and headed in that direction, which took me past the adoption center. Bob and I used to joke about the adoption center. We always looked at the cats there, always fell briefly in love with one or two. But we treasured the balance we had with our two cats and couldn't imagine having more. We always somehow willed ourselves to walk away.

So I gazed quickly over at the adoption center cages as I hurried past. Then, suddenly, out of the corner of my eye, something brought me to an abrupt halt. There was a cat—an adult cat—like none other I had ever seen. She was gorgeous. She looked vaguely Siamese, with a cream-colored body and bright blue eyes. But her face mask and ears were a startling apricot color. Her fluffy tail was a cream-and-orange-striped tabby. As I drew closer, I could see that she had a peachy cast to her largely cream-white body. She looked at me with a warmth and intelligence that was arresting. She put her paws through the cage, reaching in my direction. Her eyes never leaving mine, she gave a musical little trill. I was hooked.

Reading the information card attached to her cage, I saw that her name was Marina. She was a flame-point Siamese, a hybrid cat that is a cross between a Siamese and a red tabby. She was not quite two years old and already had been given up by two families: one because they had a baby and the baby turned out to be allergic to cats and the other because they deemed her "too needy" to be an acceptable pet for the family. She looked at me with huge, pleading blue eyes and wrapped a soft paw around my finger. When the attendant opened her cage, she leaped into my arms and started purring, burrowing her head against my cheek.

She cried when the attendant returned her to the cage. "You can't adopt her tonight anyway," she said. "You have to wait until a volunteer from her sponsoring rescue organization is here. Here's the number to call for an appointment. They require a face-to-face interview and screening."

I glanced at the card she handed me and pocketed it. I asked about kitty grass. They had none. Then I told the attendant that I would like to have my husband see Marina before we made any decision about calling the rescue organization. She nodded.

I raced out to the parking lot and tapped on the driver's-side window. Bob slowly opened his eyes and rolled the window down. "What?" he asked, guessing that the excitement on my face had nothing to do with kitty grass.

"There is this beautiful, wonderful cat I want you to see," I told him.

He grimaced. "Oh, no! Things are perfect as they are. We don't need another cat."

Then he looked more closely at my face, sighed, and opened the door.

Bob, too, was entranced by Marina. She cuddled and trilled and purred as he held her. "We've never adopted an adult cat to bring into a multicat household," he told the attendant. "How does that work? Can it work?"

The attendant nodded. "Oh, yes," she said. "Of course, you have to do it carefully, gradually, keeping her in a separate room for a week or two until they all get used to the idea and the scents of each other."

Bob sighed. "Okay," he said. "We'll call the rescue organization. We'd really like to adopt her."

When we met with the volunteer the next night, she was stern, giving us hypothetical vignettes about cat care and discipline and listening carefully to our answers. She informed us that Marina's microchip listed the rescue organization as the ultimate contact in case she was lost and that we were always answerable to the organization for her care. We assured her that we had long experience with cats, that our cats were very much a part of the family, that we would exercise care and patience in introducing her to our two other cats. I asked about testing—had she tested negative for feline leukemia and FIV? Was she up to date on vaccinations?

The volunteer was brusque. "Of course," she said, handing me Marina's medical record sheet.

We signed, scooped Marina up, and took her home, sneaking her into the second bathroom—all set up for her comfort over the next week or two—and closed the door.

We had expected a lot of curiosity and sniffing under the door. What we hadn't anticipated was the growling. This was growling beyond anything we had heard before. It was the growling of a junkyard dog. It was Maggie, her face planted in the crack under the bathroom door, for hours at a time, day and night. Who knew that our sweet little Bombay could growl like a Rottweiler? Hour after hour, day after day, the growling became the backdrop, the theme music, for our daily life.

When Maggie would leave her post to use the cat box or to eat, we would rush into the bathroom to attend to Marina's needs and cuddle her. She seemed unaffected by the growling—purring, trilling, always happy to see us, content in her surroundings.

Gus, too, seemed sanguine about the situation. He would occasionally put a paw under the door and flip on his back and look under the crack to catch a glimpse of what was within. Then he would lose interest and stroll away.

But Maggie was relentless. The growling stretched into the second week until Bob had finally had enough.

"This isn't working," he said at last. "I don't think it's ever going to work. Maggie is still so upset, and poor Marina may spend the rest of her life locked up in that bathroom. It isn't right. It isn't fair. I think we need to take her back."

I was aghast. *Take her back? And be the third family to give this wonderful cat up?* But I could see Bob's point. This was unprecedented and quickly becoming unbearable. "Let me call and talk to the rescue group," I said. "Maybe there's something more we can do to ease the situation."

Bob looked skeptical.

I called and left a message at the rescue organization. I called a cat-loving friend.

"You may have to return her," my friend said. "I think Bob is right. Sometimes it just doesn't work out, and that's such a shame. She sounds like a wonderful cat. But it all sounds so disruptive when things were going so smoothly before. You just have to accept that things don't always work out with cats."

I was thinking my friend's advice over when our brusque volunteer from the rescue group called back. "You haven't given it enough time," she said. "The minimum adjustment is one to two weeks. Just hang in through this week and see how it goes. Take the towel Marina has been lying on and give it to Maggie. Let her get used to the scent. Marina is a dream in terms of getting along with other cats. She's an absolute sweetheart. As soon as Maggie starts to calm down, things will be fine. Just give her more time."

We hunkered down for the duration . . . and within a few days, the growling diminished, then stopped. The sniffing under the door seemed friendlier. Following closely, we finally let Marina out of the bathroom. She trotted cheerfully around the house, exploring, Maggie following, with her nose planted firmly in Marina's rear end. Marina ignored her, stopping in the kitchen to nibble some treats from Maggie's bowl, and finally settling into Gus' cherished bed, placed at a corner on the living room couch. Gus was unperturbed as he wandered into the living room and stood on his hind legs to look at Marina. He started to purr. She looked at him calmly, with interest.

Then Gus moved to lick her face, and Marina suddenly hissed and swatted him. Gus flew back, stunned, then ambled out of the room.

Maggie sat watching for a minute or two more and then followed Gus. The two curled up together on the bed for a nap.

Marina had officially joined the household.

Her relationship with Maggie and Gus was cordial, but a bit distant. There was no more growling, no more hissing. But while Maggie and Gus enthusiastically groomed each other and happily shared food, Marina didn't participate in such camaraderie. She would lie close to them on the bed for hours at a time. She would eat quietly and without incident from a bowl beside theirs in the kitchen. But she groomed herself and ate only what was in her bowl, and the others respected this distance. We were later to be thankful for the distance—but now we were simply grateful that the growling had stopped and that Marina was settling in.

I was much relieved as I watched this restoration of domestic peace. Marina needed us—needed a stable, forever home where she was accepted as she was. We never saw her as too needy. While she kept a polite distance from Maggie and Gus, she quickly snuggled with us at every opportunity. She loved her people.

She enjoyed not simply her primary people but others as well. When my sister Tai, a longtime cat lover with multiple cats of her own, visited from Seattle, she spent much of the week she was with us cuddling Marina. Tai had been a favorite of Timmy's and had weathered numerous nights in bed with him chewing her hair. He had been obsessed with Tai's hair.

Marina had no obsessions. She simply loved to cuddle and would gently nudge my sister for attention. "I just love this little kitty," Tai would say, holding her, hugging her. "She's so loving, so gentle. How could anyone give her up? I'm telling you, if anything ever happens where you can't keep her, give her to me. We're buddies."

But Marina was my buddy, too. She not only shared our bed but also slept on my pillow, curled around my head, purring me to sleep. She loved to sit on Bob's lap or beside him as he read in the evenings. She loved to be held, to be cuddled and kissed. I would carry her around with me as I did household chores and fixed a late dinner after getting home from my private practice or from UCLA. More often than not, when I opened the door leading from the garage, she was waiting. She would trill and do a little dance of joy and scramble into my waiting arms.

The loss of Timmy was still very much with us, with me. But it was impossible to be sad for very long with Marina around. She trilled and sang and kissed us, delighted to be part of our family. It felt wonderful to bury my face in her soft fur at the end of a long day of working and commuting and feel her purring. My blood pressure dropped. My spirits soared, even after the most difficult of days.

She needed me.

I needed her.

She was my own personal therapy cat.

Nine:

A SECOND MIRACLE

arina was purring, curled up in the wire in-box on my home office desk while I immersed myself in paperwork. I smiled at her and remembered. Timmy used to curl up in that same in-box sometimes when he worked with me at my private practice. It was funny and somehow comforting to see another cat, at a vastly different time, curl up to keep me company as I worked.

I looked at the clock. It was half an hour until the two Joes—a contentious father and son—were due in for an emergency session.

I sat back for a minute and sighed. These two clients were likeable people and they truly loved each other. Joe Sr. was a local physician; Joe Jr., an often sullen but also slyly funny sixteen-year-old. They had been on a good run lately, with two months of relative peace between them before this latest eruption. I tried to meditate a bit and relax for the session ahead. It took a lot of energy to work with the two Joes.

A knock on the door interrupted my meditation. The Joes had arrived early. I smiled and invited them into the office and said we'd get started as soon as I took Marina back into the main part of the house.

She loved hanging out with me when I was writing or doing therapy notes, but I was always careful to remove her before clients came. I had no thoughts of trying her out as a therapy cat in these last months of my private practice. I didn't want my practice—by now based in my home office—to become any more informal than it was.

But today, Marina had other ideas. When I picked her up, she clung to the in-box, lifting it up with her and mewing piteously. "Come on, Marina," I whispered as Joe Jr. snickered. "You need to leave."

"Oh, let her stay. We don't mind," Joe Sr. said. I turned to him, still holding the cat who was grasping the in-box.

"Truly?" I asked. I looked at Marina. "Just this once . . . okay, Marina?" I set her and the in-box down on my desk and turned to the two Joes.

The session started quietly enough, but it soon escalated as the two argued about limits and house rules and parental expectations. As the shouting began I moved to intervene, bringing the conversation down to a level where each could truly hear the other. But before I could jump in, Marina was on her feet and running toward Joe Sr. She was on his lap in an instant, trilling and rubbing, interrupting his shouts. He looked down at her with astonishment. "Well, what do we have here?" he said, smiling. She rubbed against his hand, looked up at him, and trilled happily.

Then she hopped off his lap and ran across the room to Joe Jr., who was sitting on a small couch. She jumped up to the top of the couch, walking across it until she reached him. Then she curled up by his head and rubbed his left ear with her furry face, purring loudly. Forgetting his anger for a moment, Joe Jr. turned to Marina, laughing, and stroked her soft fur. "Look at her!" he said. "She's trying to make peace."

I smiled. "She has made you both smile and lower your voices," I said. "Let's continue your conversation at this level, with this little sense of good feeling, and see what we can do to resolve things."

It worked well. Marina stayed by Joe Jr., nuzzling his face when his voice began to rise in anger once again. And then again. After Marina's third intervention, he laughed. "She's reminding me to talk in a normal tone of voice," Joe Jr. said. "I really think she is. That's so weird and so amazing. Maybe I need her here all the time to keep reminding me!"

His father laughed, too. "Maybe she needs to be our therapy cat," he said. "You used to have a therapy cat in your practice, didn't you? I vaguely remember its picture on your other office bulletin board. Is this the same cat? I think this little cat could help us remember not to scream at each other. You intervene well, but she has a special touch. I couldn't help but smile at that sweet little cat with the big blue eyes."

I nodded. "If it would help you, of course we could try it," I said. "I did have a therapy cat once. His name was Timmy, and he was wonderful with the clients who chose to work with him. This is Marina. I never imagined she would be a therapy cat, but she does seem very drawn to the two of you. I'd be happy to have her here the next time you come in."

"How does that sound to you, Marina?" Joe Jr. asked quietly, holding Marina's paw.

She looked at him for a moment. Then she put her head in his hand, purring.

And so Marina became a therapy cat.

Ten:

MARINA,
THE THERAPY CAT

nce Marina was set to help the two Joes keep from escalating in volume and nonproductive fury during sessions, I let other clients know that she was available for animal-assisted therapy. Four client groups chose to work with her during those last eight months of my private practice.

Once again, I set a special day and times for animal-assisted therapy —again a Saturday with Chloe, who continued to be allergic to cats, as my first client before Marina set foot on the premises.

Marina's involvement brought a new energy to a practice that had been focused on endings and good-byes. She was bright and cheerful, sweet and energetic. She brought a youthful spirit to the room. She had a kitten's energy and curiosity, but the peaceful presence of a mature cat. She was a lively, loving two-year-old—and a perfect match for her new roster of clients.

Marina and the Two Joes: Speaking Softly for Warm Connection

The two Joes were a remarkable contrast the minute they walked in the room.

Joe Sr., a successful local physician, was always in a suit and tie, on his way to a half day of Saturday appointments at his medical office half a mile away. He was tall, lean, and athletic, his graying temples the only evidence that he was nearing sixty. He was full of energy and excitement with an impressive array of interests, from running to motorcycle racing and sailing. His gentle devotion to his family was evident as his voice always softened when he spoke of his love for his wife and son.

Joe Jr., at sixteen, was small and slim with spiky black hair and an array of well-worn T-shirts featuring his favorite bands. Music was a passion: he had a garage band and loved playing keyboards and guitar. He composed songs and bits of classical music. He also dabbled in video and film production on his home computer. He had big dreams.

The conflict between father and son was most often sparked by disagreements over that area of life between dreams and their realization: that area of paying dues, building a foundation for one's passion and work, beginning to make one's way in the world.

Marina had a method for brokering peace between the father and the teenage son. She would land on the lap or on the shoulder of whomever started a conflict or was shouting the loudest.

"The person who leaves here with the most cat fur on him is the one who most needs anger management," Joe Jr. laughed one day as they were leaving. Suddenly aghast, I stared at Joe Sr. He was the clear winner. I raced to get an adhesive roller for him to tidy up before he left.

"It's not my temper," he said, rolling and picking off the tufts of white fur clinging to his dark pants. "It's just that Marina likes to sit and to roll around on my lap to calm me down. She never sits on my son's lap. Have you noticed? Wherever he sits—in the chair over there or on the couch—she always jumps to his shoulder and rubs his face. She has such a routine going with us!"

I had noticed that Marina was quick to sit on the older Joe's lap. I thought that she might be picking up on his gentle caring, his warmth and empathy—clear even when he was expressing angry feelings—making his lap a place that felt safe, even when she was helping him to deal with his anger. Joe Jr. had a bit more of an edge. Perhaps she sensed that, too, and chose to keep a little more distance.

Watching Marina keep up a sometimes frantic pace—dashing from one to another with the two Joes—I worried about her at first, wondering if her desire to make peace stemmed from long-ago conflicts in another family, one of the families that had given her up. I worried that this might be too stressful for her. But the stress didn't appear to linger with her when their voices dropped to a conversational tone.

Marina sat curled cheerfully on my desk, watching the Joes get ready to leave and chirping, hoping to get one last pat from them. Joe Sr. went over and stroked her fur, taking care not to stand too close and get covered once again. "Thank you, Marina," he said and then, glancing at me, he sighed, "We make progress."

Indeed they were making progress, but it wasn't easy for either of them. Joe Sr. had overcome incredible odds—a difficult childhood with a grieving, hardworking widowed mother, the father who had died too early for him to remember, the early difficulties in school due to a childhood learning disorder, the hard work and persistence that led him to medical school and to a career as a successful, deeply caring physician.

Joe Sr. wanted life to be easier for his own child. He treasured his relationship with his engaging, hardworking wife, who was also a medical professional, and with this gifted but often unmotivated son. He encouraged Joe Jr.'s interests and talents in the arts but grew impatient with his lack of momentum in finishing school and finding a path to his future.

The son was bright and funny and loved his dad dearly. He could also bring him to the screaming point with his claims of genius and his disinclination to give any thought to starter jobs that could give him experience in the highly competitive field he hoped to enter. He envisioned starting at the top. Period. He saw little point in studying anything that was not an avid interest and had dropped out of high school, got his GED, and was taking classes, when the spirit moved him, at a local community college.

Marina had her work cut out for her—rushing from one to the other as they argued in sessions about motivation, consideration (Joe Jr. had a distressing habit, as he lounged around the house while his parents were at work, of leaving dishes, laundry, and other messes for them to clean up after a long day of work), and preparation (or lack of it) for the bright artistic future this young man envisioned.

As the Joes talked, Marina helped them to stay calm and listen to each other as we dealt with issues from encouraging versus enabling, aspiration versus entitlement, and the fact that love, anger, and expectations can coexist.

While we talked, Marina would sit waiting, on alert, for the next raised voice, the next eruption.

As time went on, her interventions became more widely spaced and she seemed content to sit by my side for most of the sessions.

"Look at that!" Joe Sr. exclaimed after one session near the end of our work together. "I don't need the roller at all. Not a trace of Marina on my suit today."

He came over and stroked her head. "You know what? It kind of makes me sad, Marina." She looked up at him and trilled softly.

The two Joes were chuckling as they left, the father's arm affectionately draped around his son's shoulders.

Marina and the Andersons: Finding Peace in Compromise

Carolyn and Frank Anderson were a long-married couple in crisis. Once high school sweethearts, they had married at twenty and lived as many young couples of their time with Carolyn quitting her secretarial job when their first child was born and Frank supporting the family through the years with his job as an auto mechanic. Life had been good for them: their children grew and prospered, and their modest suburban home was a warm, cozy sanctuary for family and friends.

But now this comfortable, familiar way of life was about to change. With Frank nearing retirement, with their three children grown and living at a distance, they were dealing with their upcoming changes in vastly different ways. Frank was looking forward to new freedom and adventures while Carolyn mourned what once was and dreaded the prospect of constant togetherness.

"I love my husband. I do," she would insist, tugging at the tunic of her pantsuit as she shifted uneasily in her chair. "But he can drive me crazy with his constant bossing and endless suggestions for how I can do my work and live my life better. I have this vision of him telling me how to do the housework I've been doing unaided all these years. I've seen this with the husbands of my friends. Once they retire, they become total experts at housework efficiency. Mind you, they don't participate in any of this. They just tell their wives how to do it better. And they want their meals three times a day, right on time.

Frank will have more free time and I'll have less. That's how I see it. And it's true that I miss the life we used to have. I miss the kids and the grandkids. They all live too far away to see on a regular basis. I just feel sad, like a major part of my life is over and that I don't have a lot to look forward to."

Frank broke in impatiently from across the room. "I get so tired of this down attitude of hers!" he said. "I've worked so hard to get to retirement, and I want to enjoy myself. I want us to have a good life now that we have more time together. I want to take all those driving trips we never had the time or resources to take before. We can even act like tourists in our own town. We can enjoy coffee together at 10 AM on a weekday. We could have a great life in retirement. But she's always looking at the glass half empty and acts like it's going to be a giant problem having me around more. Excuse me?" His eyes narrowed as he glared across the room at his wife of forty-five years.

As Carolyn cried quietly into her crumpled tissues, Marina stirred, rushing from the in-box on my desk to Carolyn's ample lap where she settled in, leaning against Carolyn and purring.

"Aw . . . ," Carolyn blew her nose into the tissue and looked down at Marina. "What a sweet kitty. She feels so good on my lap."

"It feels good to make a warm connection, to just sit and enjoy the moment, doesn't it?" I asked her. She nodded, petting Marina.

"I know you've been grieving the part of your life that now feels so far in the past," I said. "What about things that please you right now and that could be positives for the future?"

"Besides Marina?" she asked, with the trace of a smile. "I might enjoy having a little dog who could travel with us, maybe to see family, maybe on one of Frank's driving trips. I'd like to take a class in watercolors or get back into sewing and crafts. I'd like that."

"She says that now," Frank said, his voice rising. "But when it comes time to take a trip, she doesn't want to go. She wants to hang around the house and mope. And I don't find the idea of traveling with a dog, little or otherwise, particularly appealing."

Marina launched herself off Carolyn's lap and headed for Frank, standing up on her hind legs, planting her front legs on his knees and looking at him thoughtfully.

He stared down at her with faint disapproval. "What?" he said. "What does she want?"

"She wants you to stop shouting at and about me and to be nicer," Carolyn snapped.

Marina turned her head and looked at Carolyn.

"I think she would like both of you to take a breath, calm down, and speak with each other in a more supportive way," I said quietly.

Frank leaned back in his chair. "Oh, for Chrissakes," he muttered. "I'm supposed to take directions from a goddamned cat?"

"She's not the boss," I said. "She's just a reminder. Let's see how it goes when we just talk about what it would take for both you and Carolyn to be happy and to feel content with each other in this new phase of your life."

And so we talked as Marina listened, snuggled with Carolyn, and fixed Frank with a stare when he started to raise his voice.

In the weeks that followed, we began to make progress in planning a retirement that would work for both of them. Once the sale of Frank's auto repair business was complete and he and Carolyn were officially retired, we talked about finding ways that they could give each other space as well as support.

"Let's think about what it means for both of you to be retired," I suggested one day.

"Frank, you're really enjoying sleeping in and having that 10 AM coffee and planning those road trips. What would it mean for Carolyn to have fewer responsibilities and more fun? Any ideas?"

Frank rubbed his mustache as he always did when he was thinking. "Well, I kind of get where you're going with this," he said slowly. "So maybe if I help out with cleaning the house or with the dishes, she'd have a little more free time, too?" He grimaced. The idea didn't please him.

"Well, maybe," I said. "Instead of telling her your ideas for more efficiency in household tasks, you could show her what you mean— and also cut down on the time when she's working so that you both could have more fun together. What do you think?"

"I'd feel better if we could work together," Carolyn said slowly, watching her husband closely. "I might really get into playing together if I didn't feel that all the drudge work was still all mine."

Frank bristled. "Drudge work?" he roared. "You ought to try—" He caught Marina looking at him sadly and stopped, exasperated. "Jeez, three females in this room. I can't win."

"Is it about winning?" I asked. "Or are we trying to find a new way of being together that will help you both to have more fun and freedom in retirement?"

The room was silent for a minute. Then Marina put her paws on Frank's knees and looked at him, purring softly. Slowly, he smiled. "More fun and freedom would work for me," he said at last.

"Me, too," said Carolyn as Marina ran to curl into her lap and as we began to discuss the patterns of thinking that led to much of Carolyn's depression—focusing so much on how life used to be rather than how wonderful it could be now.

As we continued to talk and plan, working out their lifestyle compromise, Marina kept busy scurrying between Carolyn and Frank, keeping peace when tempers flared, watching happily as they took their first steps toward compromise.

We knew we had made progress and that their sessions were nearing the end when Marina would spend whole sessions sitting happily by my side, curled up, purring, perfectly content. The end of their treatment was peaceful, with smiles and plans for travel.

"She's yours again," Carolyn said, stroking Marina's head as they paused to say good-bye after their last session and as they prepared to set off on their first road trip with their new rescue dog, Pancho.

"He's my buddy," Frank said, bending down to pet the tan mongrel with the gentle, sparkling eyes and rapidly wagging tail. "He's a great hiking dog and no trouble at all on the road. And he doesn't give me any guff."

He shot a look at Marina, who sat in her in-box, tucked into my office bookshelf, surveying the scene and purring.

Marina, Lisa, and Caitlin: Rediscovering Love

L isa and Caitlin were the only new clients I accepted in my last year of practice, only because they were close relatives of another longtime patient who begged me to take them on. The only time slot I had available was on Saturday, my therapy cat day, in the middle of a schedule that had Marina working with the clients before and after them.

"My therapy cat will be in the office at that time," I told Lisa when she was scheduling the appointment. "Do you or your daughter have allergies or aversions to cats?"

There was a pause and a sigh. "No to both," Lisa said. "I guess we'd be okay with a cat around. But our insurance is paying for therapy with you, right? And the cat is just an extra? Is that how it works? And the cat's just around—not all over us? Is that the plan?"

"That's the plan," I told her, after a moment's hesitation. Marina loved cuddling with clients. But when she sensed reserve on a client's part, she would often hesitate and be watchful before getting too close.

Marina's action plan with Lisa, a trim, businesslike forty-two-year-old real estate agent, and her angry, sullen sixteen-year-old daughter, Caitlin—who tried to hide her feelings behind her great cascade of curly auburn hair that hung in her face—was immediately clear:

Marina offered her services as a living, breathing buffer between the two as they sat tight-lipped and fuming on the couch together.

Marina sat close, but not too close, and watched Lisa carefully.

"We've just been approved for six sessions by the insurance company," Lisa said. Her tone was crisp, her manner brusque. "So we don't have time to go back to our childhoods or try any New Age-y stuff or spend a lot of time playing with this cat. We need answers and a plan. That's it."

Her daughter sank into the sofa cushions, her expression dark, her left hand resting firmly on Marina's back as the cat sat between her and her mother.

"So what would you like most to accomplish during these six sessions?" I asked.

"We need to find out what's going on with Caitlin," her mother said. "She's so irritable and hard to deal with. Even her friends can't stand her. She never sees them anymore. And her grades have fallen from a 3.8 to mostly Cs this year. She won't talk to me. And I can't seem to get through to her how important it is to keep her grades up. She'll be applying for colleges in another six months! And where does a C student end up going?

"I'm angry and I'm—"

Her voice caught. "I'm concerned," Lisa said, suddenly fighting tears. "I know something is wrong, but I can't seem to help her."

Caitlin picked up Marina and held her close, seeking comfort, seeking to close out the rest of the world.

"Is there anything you would like to say right now?" I asked her quietly. She shook her head and buried her face in Marina's soft fur.

Lisa sighed and sat back, staring at me with her arms crossed. "So what now?" she asked.

It seemed more a challenge than a question.

I told her that I wasn't making assumptions until Caitlin began to feel comfortable enough to talk about her feelings, but that, quite often, teenagers who were irritable, who withdrew from friends, and who started struggling in school turned out to have significant depression. This depression could come from a major loss, some changes within the family, or even from an illness or infection.

Caitlin looked at her mother and then at me. "I did have mono last fall," she said. "It was hard because I was so tired and it put me behind in some of my classes. I haven't felt the same since."

Lisa pursed her lips. "Excuses," she said.

"It might be worth a visit to Caitlin's physician just to see how she's doing in her recovery and also to see if he or she feels whether medication might be helpful," I said. "If she does feel depressed, it could be linked to her illness last fall."

Caitlin looked into Marina's eyes and whispered, "I thought I was going crazy."

It was the beginning of an exchange of feelings and emotions that brought mother and daughter together once again. Caitlin's medical doctor agreed that her depression might have originated with her illness the previous fall and prescribed an antidepressant.

Gradually, as Marina leaned, purring, on Caitlin's chest or edged closer to—but not too close to—Lisa, mother and daughter began to talk with each other. They talked about Caitlin's discomfort with parental expectations that she apply to and, they hoped, attend their top-rated, highly competitive alma mater on the East Coast and her desire to stay at home and attend a local community college for at least the first year after high school.

"But there are so many opportunities when you attend a top college," Lisa said.

Caitlin looked down at her hands and spoke quietly. "I don't feel ready," she said. "I don't want to live away from home yet. I don't want to be away from my friends. I don't like competition. I just want a nice life." She looked up and caught her mother's skeptical look and shrugged, lapsing into uneasy silence.

Lisa's face softened. "I want you to have a nice life, too, honey," she said. "I guess maybe we need to talk about our different ideas about what makes for a nice life. I see all the opportunities out there for girls today and I want you to have . . . everything that's possible."

Hugging Marina and looking at her mother with new warmth, Caitlin's voice was soft: "I know you do, Mom, and I appreciate it," she said. "But right now, what I need is staying home, being near you and Dad and my friends as I start college. Maybe later, when I feel ready, I'll make a different choice."

Lisa took a breath, ready to argue, then caught herself and nodded. It was a new skill they were both learning: making room with silence for feelings and secrets to be shared.

Lisa began to understand that some of Caitlin's depression—and her falling grades—may not just have stemmed from her mononucleosis but also from stress over the clash of her parents' expectations with her own desires to stay close and feel safe. But, in the process, they exchanged words of frustration, disappointment, anger, exasperation, and love.

They used Marina in a game of their own invention to cut down on interruptions: the person touching Marina—still sitting between mother and daughter during their sessions—had the floor. The other person had to stroke Marina's head before speaking. It was a game both agreed was silly, but it did remind each to take a breath and to listen before responding.

And Marina luxuriated in a lot of attention those last few sessions!

At their sixth and last session, mother and daughter agreed that they were much closer to a mutual understanding and that Caitlin's depression was beginning to lift.

"We just need to remember our game with Marina and keep talking without interrupting each other," Lisa said, squeezing her daughter's hand.

Caitlin smiled slyly. "Maybe we need to get a cat."

Lisa rolled her eyes. "We definitely need to talk," she said. And then she laughed.

Marina and the Morelli Family: Listening, Hearing, Understanding

The Morelli family was Marina's ultimate challenge. They were loving and angry, occasionally outrageous, and always loud—and there were a lot of them.

There was Nana Maria, Mr. Morelli's widowed mother who lived with the family and who, in her early eighties, was suffering from some cognitive deficits. But that didn't slow down her lively stream of opinions and observations or still her full-throated brays of laughter. Her parents had been Italian immigrants, and Maria was born and raised in New York City. Traces of the city were still evident, especially when she was excited or angry. She had firm opinions about how her grandchildren should be raised and behave, which brought her nose to nose at times with her daughter-in-law Patti, a frazzled, beleaguered woman in her midforties who combined a part-time catering business with raising four children, now all in various stages of adolescent angst.

Mark, the forty-six-year-old son, husband, and father, was a prominent local attorney and often felt caught in the middle of the battles between his wife and his mother. "There's nothing I see in the courtroom that begins to rival what I see at home," he told me with a touch of weariness and resignation.

Eldest child Danielle, seventeen, was the only quiet member of the family. She often sealed herself off with ear buds and an MP3 player to do homework and otherwise escape the ongoing family chaos. She dreamed of attending college on the East Coast, as far away from the family as she could get. Her parents strongly wished otherwise: that she would continue to live at home, commute to UCLA, and keep up her participation in the family drama.

Luke, sixteen, the only son, was a risk-taker, dabbling in everything from marijuana to extreme skateboarding, drinking, partying, and spending as little time as possible doing either homework or housework. While his drug and alcohol use were light and only occasional, it provided ample fodder for family conflicts.

Tracy, fourteen, was a jock, a tall, slender young woman with dreams of continuing to play basketball and soccer through high school and college and, perhaps, beyond. She was in constant motion, feet, hands, legs—all moving to an unheard rhythm as she struggled to sit still in therapy sessions that she loudly proclaimed that she, above all, did not need.

Donna, thirteen, did everything full out—arguing, crying, lapsing into stormy silences. The other members of the Morelli family referred to her as the "drama queen," but Donna contended that she was simply trying to be heard and understood in a family that tended to shout and argue at full volume constantly, giving equal emotional weight to all problems whether small or major.

There were three generations under one roof and crowding into the therapy room—sometimes all together, sometimes in pairs, as triplets or quartets.

Whatever the combination, sessions were never dull. They railed and roiled through their amped-up versions of more or less typical parent-child conflicts: differing goals and expectations, concerns over drug and alcohol use, indifference to academics, lack of foresight and motivation. The youngest generation's attempts at individuation often clashed with the older generations' concept of family unity. Patti and Maria aired their child-raising differences loudly and often. Mark would try to make peace, then lose his patience and outshout everyone. If not carefully monitored and contained, therapy with the Morellis could be a donnybrook.

The family had come to therapy a number of times, on an as-needed basis as crises came up over the past several years. While they had been clients when Timmy was the resident therapy cat in my professional office, they had never seen him. The family preferred weekday evening appointments, and at the time I couldn't have imagined adding a cat—even a cat as unflappable as Timmy—to the volatile mix at sessions that more often than not included the whole family.

But the options were fewer once I moved my practice to my smaller home office during a time when the Morelli family was on hiatus from therapy. When they called back in crisis a few months after the move, I tried to steer them to another therapist. No dice. "We don't want to start over with someone else right now," Patti insisted. "We tried that other woman you suggested—terrible. She spent the whole time telling us to shut up and never hearing what we were saying. This is just one problem—well, maybe two—that we need to handle. Can't we come for even a few sessions?"

My home office couldn't easily accommodate the whole family. We compromised with a quartet to begin: Mark, Patti, Danielle, and Luke. It became a quintet when Mark hesitated to leave his mother alone at home with the two younger daughters. The only day all were available was Saturday.

I warned them that they were coming on my therapy cat day—asking if there would be a problem with allergies or aversions or whether they might welcome a bit of feline intervention.

Patti hesitated at the prospect of adding wildlife to the already semiferal family mix. "Well," she said, "we're sort of dog people more than cat people. But maybe it could work. Let's try it. I can't imagine a cat helping us, but it wouldn't be a problem either. We'll probably scare the poor thing out of the room."

Marina did sit back with uncharacteristic reticence as the Morelli quintet squeezed into the room, already squabbling and shouting. Her blue eyes scanned the visitors with wonder as she settled at my feet, watchful and waiting.

I set the ground rules once again: airing feelings was fine, but I would intervene if people weren't hearing each other for the shouting. This session would not be simply high-volume venting but would be working toward some new understanding and solutions. To do that, we would need to listen to each other, tone down the volume, and respect each others' opinions and suggestions.

There was the usual collective sigh as we began—and before long, Mark, Patti, Luke, and Maria were actively trading shouts and insults while Danielle fell into sullen silence, rolling her eyes heavenward. As I started my referee intervention, Marina suddenly sprang to life, running into the center of the room with a series of chirps and trills. She jumped at invisible prey. She chased her tail. She ran in full circles around the room, pouncing on someone's foot here, tapping another's leg there. The shouting stopped as the family stared in confusion and amusement.

"What is that cat doing?" Danielle asked, a little uneasy.

Good question. I watched Marina continue to dash around, jumping and tapping and trilling.

"I think she's trying to distract you and help you to calm down," I said at last.

Mark laughed mirthlessly. "With all that hyperactivity she's trying to calm us down?"

"Well, listen and look," I said. "You're all quiet now. Watching her. When was the last time that happened? Maybe if we all keep talking in this tone, we can resolve some of your issues here and give Marina a rest."

They agreed, working out a new after-school schedule for Luke and hearing Danielle's desire for greater independence without screaming or judgments. Marina curled up at my feet and napped.

It had been a good session.

The family agreed that Marina's intervention had been effective— and something entirely new that had shocked them into silence. The question remained: Would it work again?

The next session was a triple—with Mark, Patti, and Maria. They kept their voices low and their anger well contained, keeping an eye on Marina, who roosted on my desk, surveying the scene. Only toward the end did the debate veer toward chaos, with Maria beginning to shout her frustration at new constraints and indignities. She was angry about Mark hiding the car keys from her and asking her not to cook unless someone else was helping in the kitchen.

Marina jumped off the desk and ran over to Maria, chirping, trilling, and prancing around her feet. Maria continued to shout. Marina started running in tight circles again, chasing her tail. She fell to the ground and wiggled at Maria's feet.

Maria was still angry, but she lowered her voice. "My whispering is the only thing that will stop this nonsense," she said, glaring down at Marina.

And she was right.

As we talked in low voices, the Morelli family began to make a working plan to regulate their changing life, given Maria's recent diagnosis of dementia. "The issue as I see it isn't a matter of power and restrictions, but a plan for keeping you safe, Mom," Mark said quietly. "We love you. We want to be sure that you're safe."

Maria looked as if she were about to start shouting again, but one glance in Marina's direction changed that. Maria's lower lip trembled a little as she looked over at her son. "But I'm fine," she said. "No matter what the doctor said. I'm just fine. There's no reason why I—"

She broke off, startled by the sudden tears in her son's eyes and the catch in her own throat. She shrugged. "Oh, well," she said, with a sideways look at Marina. "If it means you won't worry, okay. I don't want you to worry."

Mark crossed the room to embrace his mother. Patti rubbed Maria's shoulder as they huddled quietly, brought together with love and a new appreciation for quiet resolution of differences.

Marina broke the silence with a small, satisfied trill and climbed onto my lap for a well-earned nap.

MARINA'S ENDURING LESSONS FOR PATIENTS—AND FOR ME

In her short but memorable turn at being a therapy cat, Marina taught some important lessons to my patients and to me:

❖ **Let silence build an alliance.** There are all kinds of silences. Some are sullen or stony and block communication. But a warm silence, the silence that comes from listening and really hearing another, from taking the time to look into the eyes of another and see much more than you could ever learn in words, can build strong bonds with those we love. The Morelli family learned this lesson partly from Marina's firm interventions. Frank learned it when he stopped trying to win an argument and paused to listen to his wife's feelings. The skill brought Lisa and Caitlin together in a whole new way, and it resonated for me as well.

My Irish family of origin was and is highly verbal—with get-togethers filled with stories and opinions and song and debate. My husband and I, too, were attracted by each other's verbal skills. While I learned, during my clinical training, the value and necessity of warm, silent support in allowing patients to sort out their feelings and options, keeping quiet and letting the process happen was sometimes a challenge for me. Seeing the impact of silence on the garrulous Morelli clan was instructive; I vowed to value silence anew, making more quiet, pivotal moments possible.

🐾 **Remember the power of forgiveness in freeing our hearts to love.** While this was a tremendous lesson for Timmy's client Irene in letting go of her burden of bitterness toward her late husband and her resentful daughter, it made a difference to Marina's patients, too. When Lisa and Caitlin began to forgive each other for having different dreams of the future, when Frank and Carolyn forgave each other for the ways their life paths and experiences had diverged on the way to coming together again in a happy, shared retirement, then real change became possible.

No one can teach the lesson of forgiveness better than a rescue animal. No matter how many families have overlooked or rejected them, even though they may have been mishandled, abused, or abandoned, these animals are almost always willing to give humans another chance. They don't hang onto grievances. They keep themselves open and available for love.

Marina could have been the poster cat for forgiveness. She had been adopted, then abandoned by two families in the first eighteen months of her life. We long suspected, because of her unusually startled and frightened reactions to a simple reprimand, that she may have been abused in one of these homes. It was heartbreaking to imagine that her gift for quieting conflict may have developed in an angry, conflicted home at some point earlier in her life.

Marina taught me a particularly memorable lesson in forgiveness after her days as a therapy cat were over, when I left her—along with Gus and Maggie—to board at their vet's while Bob and I moved our furniture to Arizona before coming back to claim them. Marina was crushed, completely devastated at being left. She may have imagined that, once again, she was being abandoned. Also, her boarding week was a difficult one, filled with painful and scary medical tests. But when she saw me, coming back to pick her up, there was only joy. Her message, as she jumped into my arms with trills and kisses, was clear: "Oh, life is wonderful! You've come back for me!"

It made me think about how many opportunities for forgiveness we miss in our lives as we hold onto grudges, hurt feelings, the need to be right, or hasty judgments. When we forgive, we grow free of these obstacles to connection and open ourselves to new opportunities for love and happiness.

Strive to live in the present. This is another lesson we can learn from all our animal companions, but one that Marina lived with particular fervor. She lived to play, to hang out with her people, to relish her meals and revel in a warm cuddle. There were no shoulds, no tyranny of schedules with Marina. She found pleasure in every pursuit, every relationship, in her life.

Animals, quite naturally, live in the present. For humans, this skill often has to be cultivated but is well worth the effort in enabling us to savor and enjoy each moment of our lives.

Not long ago, I visited two Catholic nuns at their retirement home. Both are in their eighties and suffering from cancer. One of them, Sister Rita, is a beloved former teacher whom I have known for more than sixty years.

The other, Sister Anne, has been her close friend since their days as teenage novices back at the Motherhouse in Ireland. I expressed my surprise that, despite their illnesses, they were joyous, vibrant, and surprisingly active.

"Ah, yes, we were talking about that just before you came," said Sister Anne, smiling, the faint trace of a brogue still adding a musical lilt to her speech. "It has to do with where we live in our lives. We live most happily in the present. Today is wonderful. The past is gone. And who knows about the future? But today—today is just grand, isn't it?"

Yes. Today *is* just grand if we allow ourselves to live fully in each moment.

❖ **You can accomplish much with patience.** I often marveled at how patient Marina was with clients who were anxious or who lapsed into heated arguments repeatedly despite our best efforts. There were times when Marina would dash into the fray, seeking to comfort or distract the combatants, but at least as often she would sit calmly, with rapt attention, making eye contact as a quiet reminder, whether from across the room or sitting beside or on the lap of a client.

While I considered myself fairly mellow as a therapist and reasonably patient personally, I still had a lot to learn from my therapy cat. She made me alert to ways in which I wasn't quite as patient as I thought—a tendency to finish sentences with a person who spoke very slowly, an occasional lapse into rushing an insight or pointing out something quite obvious to me to a client who was struggling—particularly if it had been a long day and I was tired.

Timmy and Marina taught me to allow clients—and others in my life—the time to express their feelings at whatever pace, in whatever time, worked for them. And if I happened to be tired, I could use the time to offer warm support and to rest my own spirit as I sat with them.

I watched Marina staying with a patient as if time had no meaning and I began to learn how to still my own restlessness within and realized the beneficial impact this could have on the therapy process. Calm can be catching, reassuring, inspiring. Having the patience to wait for hard-won insights and long-awaited client breakthroughs can make a major difference in another's life.

● **Embrace change.** We spend so much of our lives contemplating, fearing, and resisting change. Yet in those moments when we embrace change, when we take the risk of trying something new or setting off on a road not taken, we often experience our times of greatest growth and deepest satisfaction.

Marina, in particular, taught me a lot about accepting and embracing change.

At first glance, cats would seem to be the last role models imaginable for positive change. After all, they tend to be fixed in their habits and rituals. Any deviation from these can meet with stubborn resistance and immense displeasure. Try introducing a cat to a new food or, at times, even to a new toy that you had hoped he or she would enjoy.

"Kitties hate surprises!" Bob and I will often joke when we have, by accident, bought a can of cat food with an unfamiliar taste or texture and have watched all four cats turn up their noses, or dart furtively away from a truly cool new toy.

But with major changes, cats can show incredible grace and resilience.

Looking back, I couldn't help but marvel at how quickly Marina, an adult when we adopted her, made our home her own, despite Maggie's extended growlings, despite rejection from other families. I was amazed at how gracefully she moved into her new role as a therapy cat and how happily she lived with our various moves, first to a transitional home in Los Angeles while our longtime home was being sold and then to an out-of-state new home. As long as she could be with her people and still part of the family, she was happy in any location.

Cats may be more adept than we realize about discerning the difference between a change over which they can exert some control and going with the flow into a change over which they have little, if any, control.

This point inspired me in my own struggles to develop the wisdom to tell the difference between changing what was possible and accepting what couldn't be changed and, following Marina's example, to embrace change enthusiastically as an opportunity for growth and discovery.

Marina

Maggie meets Gus

Eleven:

TRANSITION AND SHOCK

Marina ended her career as a therapy cat where she began: with the two Joes.

That last session was a peaceful one of looking back at our work together—and looking ahead: at Joe Sr.'s plan to cut back his medical practice hours and Joe Jr.'s firm plans to finish his graphic design course at the local community college. They both asked if it would be possible, if an emergency arose, to do a phone session or two. I nodded.

"Of course, a phone session wouldn't be quite the same," Joe Sr. said, stroking Marina's head. "It wouldn't include Marina. She's really special. I've enjoyed her so much."

Joe Sr. embraced me as they left and his son quickly, awkwardly, followed suit. "Have a very happy retirement you two," Joe Sr. said. "You've earned it!"

When they were gone, I picked Marina up and hugged her. "We're retired now," I told her. "You did so well, Sweetheart. Soon it will be time to relax and just enjoy our lives together." I kissed her and she began to purr.

Retirement was close, but we weren't quite there yet. I had two and a half months to go at UCLA Medical Center, and Bob was keeping his engineering job, too, until at least mid-April.

But we had made progress. We had bought a new house in Arizona the previous July and were about to put our California home on the market. Our real estate agent, a young Vietnamese woman with a towering reputation as the most aggressive salesperson in the area, was blunt: we needed to take our old furniture and our cats and vacate the premises. She preferred to sell the property vacant—after workers had completed painting, recarpeting, and ceiling scraping.

We were in shock, wondering where we would live while our house was on the market and while winding up our work lives in Los Angeles. My brother Mike came up with the solution, offering us use of his rental home in the L.A.-area town of La Cañada Flintridge. This small two-bedroom cottage had been our childhood home. Mike's most recent longtime tenant had just married and moved out, leaving much of her furniture behind. Mike offered it to us for as long as we might need it. We gratefully accepted and made plans to transport our own furniture to Arizona in advance of our final move.

Now there was only one problem to be solved: What would we do with our cats while we were moving our household belongings to Arizona? When we had gone away previously, we always had left the cats at home in the care of a professional pet-sitter. But, during this major move, crews were moving in to scrape ceilings and paint—not a healthy environment for our cats. And we didn't want to leave them at the La Cañada house, thirty miles away, a place unfamiliar to them, a place where we didn't know any pet-sitters. We turned to Dr. Tracy for help, and she was quick to offer a solution: she agreed to keep Gus, Maggie, and Marina in a special boarding area of her office during the week we would be gone.

"Don't worry about a thing," she said. "I can put them all in one kitty condo and they'll be together and can console one another. It will be fine."

We rented a moving van that would be packed by movers in California and unpacked by another set of movers in Arizona. Bob would drive the truck to our new home, and then we would drop it off at another Budget location in Arizona. I would follow him in my car.

It was all too easy. The morning of the move, we got the cats into their carriers with minimal struggles. I dropped Bob off at the truck rental facility and continued on to Dr. Tracy's.

I was filling out paperwork in the lobby, surrounded by the three cat carriers when a woman came in to purchase some prescription cat food. In passing, she peered into Marina's carrier. "Oh, my God!" she cried, smiling through sudden tears. "A flame-point! I love flame-points! They're the nicest cats in the world. I had a flame-point male for eighteen years, and I just lost him two years ago."

A tear slipped down her cheek. "There has never been another cat like him," she continued, brushing her tear away. "You're so lucky to have this one. There's really nothing like a flame-point kitty."

She touched the mesh of Marina's carrier. Marina looked at her curiously for a moment, then rubbed her face against the mesh, purring.

Just then, a technician came to review my information sheet and take Gus, Maggie, and Marina to their kitty condo. "I'll see you later, Sweethearts," I said to the cats, stepping back. They stared at me. Then Gus and Maggie turned their backs to me and hunkered down in their carriers.

But Marina's eyes grew large as she continued to look at me. She began to whimper and tremble. I realized that perhaps she thought she was being abandoned once again. I knelt down beside her carrier and started to unzip it.

"No! No, don't do that!" the receptionist said. "We don't allow open cat carriers in the lobby. She'll be okay. Really."

I stepped back and looked at Marina, concerned. The whimpering had become crying. She was shaking all over. Her eyes were pleading.

"I love you, Marina, and I'll be back for you and Maggie and Gus very soon," I said. "It will be fine. I promise. I'll see you soon."

She was inconsolable. The tech and receptionist motioned for me to go. I forced myself to leave, jumping into the car and heading back to the house, unable to shake the vision of Marina in such distress.

Half an hour later, I was standing in the driveway as the movers loaded furniture into the van when my cell phone rang. I flipped it open: it was Dr. Tracy.

"Marina has had a cardiac episode," she said. "We've revived her, but I'm concerned. She's only three years old. It isn't normal for a three-year-old otherwise healthy cat to experience cardiac distress. Would be it all right to do some tests?"

"Yes, of course," I said. "Would it help if I came back? To comfort and hold her?"

"No," Dr. Tracy said. "She would just get stressed out all over again when you left. We'll take good care of her, and I'll let you know about the tests as soon as I get the results."

My knees felt weak. I sat down in my car. Praying wasn't something I did often, but I whispered a small prayer this time: Please let Marina be all right.

"Poor little Bunny," Bob said, leaning against the car and using his favorite nickname for Marina. "She just got stressed out about being left. Let's get all this done and get back to her as soon as we can."

The seven-hour drive went smoothly. We began to relax as the Arizona moving crew finished placing the last of the furniture in our new home. I was unpacking dishes when my cell phone rang again.

It was Dr. Tracy.

"The test results are back," she said. "And I'm afraid I have some bad news. Marina has leukemia."

"Feline leukemia?" I gasped. "But the rescue organization said she had tested negative."

"Either it was a false negative or they didn't test her," Dr. Tracy said quietly. "You have kept her indoors. Neither Gus nor Maggie tests positive for leukemia. She must have had this from the beginning."

My mind raced. Feline leukemia can be contagious between cats. I was suddenly thankful that Marina had kept a polite distance from Gus and Maggie, never engaging in mutual grooming or sharing food. But my heart broke at the prospect of losing her—as I knew I would.

"How can we protect our other two cats?" I asked. "And what is her prognosis?"

There was a moment of silence on the other line. I had a sudden fear that Dr. Tracy would recommend putting Marina down to protect Maggie and Gus. I feared that she would say that Marina was actively dying.

But Dr. Tracy's answer was reassuring. "I would recommend giving Gus and Maggie a super-immunization series," she said. "That's three vaccinations over three weeks while they are kept completely separate from Marina. We've already taken her out of their condo and put her in a separate area. Her prognosis isn't good, of course. Feline leukemia is always fatal eventually. With cats infected at birth, as I believe Marina was, we lose about 20 percent of infected cats each year. Marina is three, so—"

"So we could still have a year with her? Maybe two years?" I asked, trying not to sob, wiping my tears away with the dishtowel.

Dr. Tracy was quiet for a moment and then replied, "Yes, that might be possible. I hope that's the way it goes. Let's start the immunizations for the other two now, and you need to make plans to keep them apart from Marina for three weeks. And we'll just try to keep her as stress-free as possible."

I thanked her, hung up, and embraced Bob as we both stood in our lovely new kitchen and cried.

We devised a plan for the next three weeks: we would set up litter boxes in both bedrooms of our temporary home in La Cañada. Maggie and Gus would sleep in the second bedroom and have the run of the house. Marina would take up residence in the master bedroom, spending nights with us and days napping by herself in the large sunny room.

No one was happier about this plan than Marina. She trilled with delight when we picked the cats up from Dr. Tracy's. She was even happier to have her own room—with us—when we got to La Cañada. She ran and bounced around the room with excitement and joy. I could almost hear her saying, "It has happened! My dream! I'm an only cat at last!"

Our ten weeks in La Cañada were among the happiest of her life.

Even after her happy isolation from the other cats ended, she still felt special. As Maggie and Gus, disturbed by unfamiliar scents and sights, still crawled on their bellies, cautiously, through the house, Marina pranced, chirping and trilling, spending hours perched in the bay window of the living room, waiting for us to get home from work. It was a wonderful routine: I would park my car in the drive-up parking area by the front porch and we would spot each other, she with her nose and front paws pressed against the window. Then she would disappear and be right by the front door as I came into the house, standing on her hind legs begging to be petted. Once in my arms, she would cuddle and kiss, touching noses and purring.

"I've never seen her happier," Bob said, his eyes sad. "Sweet little Bunny. She's such a joy. I hope we do get those two more years with her."

My sister Tai was somewhat less optimistic when I gave her the news. "Oh, no! Not Marina!" she cried when I told her over the phone. "That's such a terrible disease. You know, I lost several cats to leukemia before the vaccines were available. I know this may shock you, but I learned it the hard way: feline leukemia is a very slippery slope. Once a cat starts to get sick, it's all downhill. Don't get into expensive treatments. Nothing does any good. When she gets sick, when that time comes, just love her and let her go. I'm serious. That's the kindest thing. But, oh my God! Why Marina? She's so wonderful, so beautiful! I just love her so much!"

We loved her with an extra measure of affection in those days and weeks. When our home sold after only two weeks on the market to a cash buyer who wanted a thirty-day escrow, we firmed up our plans to retire and move to Arizona permanently in mid-April.

This was the move we had dreaded: in the car, with the cats for the seven-hour journey. We conferred with Dr. Tracy about how to minimize the stress for all of them, particularly for Marina.

"Keep them all in their carriers," she said. "But keep Marina close to you. Make sure she sees you at all times. Talk with her. Give her treats."

Marina loved the trip over to Arizona, chirping, trilling, and purring as she sat between us in the front seat. Maggie and Gus, in the backseat, slept most of the way.

When we got to the new house and released them from their carriers, we took them immediately to their litter boxes. But all three were more interested in exploring. And all were reassured by the familiar scents of our old furniture, their old toys, their longtime cat beds. There was no suspicious slinking, no belly-crawling, no anxiety as they settled in. They were home.

Marina seemed to be the happiest of all. Not only did she rediscover her toys and her little house atop the scratching post as well as her favorite furniture roosting points, but she also delighted in the new features our new home offered. She loved sliding on the tile floors and rolling around on the granite countertops in the kitchen (when we weren't looking) and seeking out new hiding places.

And her therapy cat skills remained. We discovered this the day after our final move when Bob received a phone call from his former workplace. Bob had spent months trying to train other employees to cover his duties and learn his accounts. He had been particularly careful to explain ongoing projects to a close coworker who was now calling with a question that revealed that he had not been paying attention at all to Bob's previous instructions.

Bob's voice began to rise, with an edge of irritability, as he spoke with this former coworker about the project. He leaned against the kitchen counter, frowning.

In an instant, Marina was beside him. She rubbed her head against his free hand and then rolled around on the countertop to distract him, eliciting a smile and helping him to keep calm throughout the call.

Bob laughed when he hung up the phone and petted her soft, furry stomach. "Still the therapy cat, aren't you, sweet Bunny!" he said. "Thanks so much."

She nuzzled him and, with a quick look in my direction, jumped off the counter.

I was thrilled with her energy and exuberance. The move hadn't seemed to stress her or exhaust her at all. She was playful and fun. She even got into trouble—a first for this sweet, dignified little cat.

It happened about a week after our move. Marina was jumping from couch to table to kitchen counter. From the kitchen counter, she decided to launch herself across the expansive entryway to a glass curio cabinet against the opposite wall. She barely made it, thumping against the display case and upsetting a row of delicate keepsakes, as she hauled herself up to the top.

"Marina!" my voice had risen in anger and alarm the minute she thumped against the case. "No!"

I stopped, suddenly ashamed. I had never yelled at Marina. Not ever. And nothing was broken, just rearranged. And even if something had been broken, so what? But I couldn't take back the angry words.

Marina was visibly crushed by the reprimand. She hung her head sadly and crept under the dining room table, curling up in a tight ball with her back to me.

"Marina, I'm sorry, Sweetheart," I said, stooping down to her under the table. She wouldn't look at me.

I extended my hand in her direction. She made no move to rub her face on it. I touched her head, and she turned her face away.

I felt terrible. How could I lose my temper with such a sweet little animal, a little cat with limited time to live, a tender soul who was so sensitive?

I decided to give her a little time and space, occasionally walking by and talking with her in soft tones, telling her that I was sorry and that I loved her.

It took several hours before she turned to face me and emerged from under the table. I stooped down to pet her and then pick her up. "I'm so sorry, Marina," I said. "I will never, ever yell at you again."

She looked at me and began to purr.

When I set her down, she went over to the display case immediately and sat by it. Catching my eye, she dropped her head.

"That's all right, Marina," I said. "I know you're sorry. And I'm sorry for yelling at you. You're such a good girl. And I love you so much."

She ran back to me for more cuddling.

As I held her, I felt a surge of gratitude for her apparent good health and abundant energy. I imagined many more cuddles and more romping and shared joy as we settled into our new home.

Marina and Bob

Gus with Kitten Maggie

Twelve:

LOSING MARINA

It was not to be. We knew that our time with Marina would be limited. We had hoped for another year, maybe two if we were lucky. But the beginning of the end showed up quietly one day not quite three weeks after our move.

Scott Denning, the salesperson who had sold us our new house, dropped by for a visit, eager to see how we were doing and how we liked the house, and to meet our cats, especially the therapy cat we had talked about so often.

"Where is she?" he asked. "Your therapy cat?"

I smiled. "Oh, she'll be here any minute," I said. "She can't stay away from visitors. She insists on being the first to greet them."

"Oh, there's a kitty," Scott said, pointing. "Is that the one?"

I turned around. It was Maggie, our black Bombay cat, who was usually shy with strangers. She walked over to Scott, rubbing against his outstretched hand. Then she hopped onto Bob's lap and settled in for a nap.

"No," I said, a little surprised that Maggie was the greeter for the day.

Marina never appeared during Scott's visit.

Something felt wrong. After he left, I looked in the bedroom. Gus was curled up on the bed asleep and alone. I searched other favorite spots. Nothing. Finally, I looked under the bed. She was there sitting quietly. She didn't seem ill. Just quiet. A little distant. I reached out to pet her, and she rubbed her face on my hand.

I decided to watch her carefully for the next day or so, monitor her food intake, and hunt up a local vet. We were still so new to the area that we were only starting to line up medical and dental professionals. I looked in my file of local services and found an ad I had clipped for Dr. Wendy Holst at Coolidge Animal Wellness Clinic. Coolidge was another small town about six miles from our home. It seemed a reasonable choice.

I called Dr. Wendy's office the next day when I noticed that Marina had not touched her food for dinner the night before or breakfast that morning. The receptionist told me that Dr. Wendy was at her Mesa office that day, but would be in Coolidge and available to see Marina the next day. "Do you feel this is an emergency?" she asked.

I sighed. "I don't know," I said. "I'm concerned that she's not eating and is so withdrawn. It's not like her at all. And I guess I'm particularly worried because she has been diagnosed recently with feline leuke-mia. Until now, she has been lively and seemed so healthy. But sud-denly, she's just different. She doesn't seem sick. Just very quiet."

We agreed on a morning appointment the next day. I spent much of the day lying on the floor by the bed, petting Marina, giving her water, watching her with concern as she sat quietly. And I was hop-ing, praying, that this wasn't the beginning of the end, the first step on that slippery slope.

Although the twinge of anticipatory loss was always present after Marina's diagnosis, it was easy to push such feelings aside, to imagine such a loss months or years in the future. She had been so exuber-ant, so happy, so lively before and after our last move. While we were beginning to accept the fact that she was going to die in young adult-hood, I couldn't quite imagine the end coming anytime soon.

But Dr. Wendy looked grave as she finished her examination of Marina and reviewed her latest lab reports with us. She pointed out a flicker of jaundice in the corners of Marina's eyes and stroked her gently as she said, "She's going into total organ failure, end-stage leu-kemia. She will probably die very soon. In fact, since you have her here today, we could—"

"Oh, no! Please no!" I was surprised by my own outburst. "I need more time with her. Just a little more time. Can't you give her any medication that would help her for just a little longer? I know it's probably selfish, but I'm not ready. I can't—"

Dr. Wendy reached over the examining table and took my hand. "It's all right," she said. "I understand. This must seem very sudden to you. And she does have a little infection. Let me give you some medication for the infection and let's see how she does. Why don't you give her the medicine and watch her over the weekend and then check back with me on Monday and we'll see how things stand?"

I was filled with gratitude. A few more days. Maybe if the infection cleared . . . maybe if I hand-fed her . . . maybe with enough love and reassurance. My mind raced with love and denial.

When we got home, we gave Marina a dose of her medication. I tried to hand-feed her a few bites of chopped chicken breast. She had no interest in food, looking at me with large, questioning eyes as I coaxed her to eat. I put her on the bed and rubbed her back, giving her sips of water and telling her how much I loved her.

Because I tend to be the family photographer, I realized that I had no pictures of myself with Marina. I asked Bob to take some of us together. They were terribly sad. Marina was compliant, resting in my arms quietly. But her joyous spirit, her loving embrace, her happy trills were gone.

By midafternoon, even I had to admit that the medication seemed to have no effect on her. She was dazed and distant. When she walked to the litter box, she seemed to stagger a little.

In her last trip to the cat box, she fell coming out of it, sliding to the floor with a startled cry and going into a seizure. Gus and Maggie were at her side in an instant, rubbing her with their faces and trying to comfort her as she writhed and cried on the floor.

Bob and I stood watching, quiet with grief.

"My poor little Bunny," Bob said, kneeling down and stroking her head. Exhausted, she looked at him and raised her chin so that he could stroke underneath.

As much as I wanted to wish it away, I knew this was the slippery slope my sister had talked about. And Marina wasn't at the top looking down. She was bottoming out.

I gently scooped her up and held her in my arms, wishing I could hold her forever, stopping time and the relentless course of this terrible disease. I tried to memorize the softness of her fur; her sweet, soft scent; the warm feel of her in my arms.

She began to whimper and seize again. I kissed her and set her down gently on the bed. Maggie and Gus jumped up to lie beside her.

I turned to Bob. "I think I need to call Dr. Wendy now," I said, barely able to speak.

"I think so, too," he said. "Do you want me to call?"

"No, I can," I said, glancing at the clock. It was 4:45 PM. I remembered that the clinic closed at five.

"It's not a problem," Dr. Wendy said softly. "We'll stay open for you. I know this is so hard and you wanted to be sure that you did everything you could for her. I really think this is the right decision, the right time. We're here for you."

Marina was so quiet in her carrier on the six-mile trip to Coolidge that I often checked to see if she was still breathing. I unzipped the top of the carrier and stroked her soft fur. I wished she would die quietly, right here, in my arms, en route to the clinic. I wished that we didn't have to make the decision that she would die today.

Bob echoed my feelings as we drove through the cotton and corn fields, resplendent with midspring green, on the way to Coolidge. Another beautiful day in May, almost three years to the day after we lost Timmy.

"I'm not sure she's going to make it to the doctor's," Bob said, reaching a hand over to touch her soft fur. "It's okay, sweet Bunny. It's okay to go now if you need to."

Marina seemed to be in a faraway place, but still conscious, when we arrived at Dr. Wendy's clinic.

"What a beautiful kitty she is," the vet tech said softly as she placed Marina on the metal examining table and prepared to put a port in her left hind leg. "And she's so good."

When she looked up, there were tears in her eyes. "I'm so sorry," she said.

Dr. Wendy came in and stroked Marina, too. "You've done all you could do for her," she said.

I couldn't speak. I just looked at Marina on that metal table. She was lying still, but she was suddenly aware, watchful. Her eyes met mine. I put my hand down to stroke her head, and with great effort she placed her head in my hand, her eyes never leaving mine. Bob stroked her tenderly. We both told her how much we loved her as Dr. Wendy inserted the needle into the port.

Marina's blue eyes continued to look into mine—as her black pupils became wider and wider, nearly blocking out the blue.

Marina died as gently as she lived, leaving this life with a little sigh.

Thirteen:

LESSONS IN GRIEF AND LOSS

I thought I knew everything there was to know about grief. I thought I was an expert. I did have experience. My parents both died of heart attacks, four months apart, when I was thirty-five. My beloved maternal grandmother died of a devastating stroke six weeks after my mother's death. My only pregnancy ended in miscarriage. A number of close friends—including three of my four college roommates—died at distressingly early ages.

But nothing quite prepared me for the loss of an animal companion.

We grieved Freddie, Timmy, and Marina in different ways. Freddie, who died at seventeen after a long decline from cancer and kidney failure, was our first cat, our only cat for all but the last few months of his life. He had a wonderful feline life as an indoor/outdoor cat, with friends—both human and feline—throughout the neighborhood. His last eight months, we had given him daily saline infusions to counteract dehydration; for all but his last few weeks, this had improved his quality of life significantly. We felt we had done everything we could to help him live fully up to his last day, yet when he died, we were grief-stricken. We astonished ourselves by crying as much over Freddie's death as we had over our parents' deaths. If we were totally honest, we may have cried a little more for Freddie.

Timmy's quick demise from melamine poisoning was traumatic for him and for us. It was forty-eight hours from first troublesome symptoms to death. Our grief was layered with fury over the corporate cost-cutting that substituted melamine for wheat products in commercial cat food. We felt guilty that we, quite unwittingly, had fed him this tainted food and that we didn't notice any symptoms until he was beyond help. To this day, any thoughts of that last, terrible time together in the euthanasia room, where Timmy desperately tried to escape, bring tears. We were devastated by his death.

Losing Marina was profoundly sad. Although we had a few months' warning that she would not live to grow old, we hadn't expected to lose her so soon. She had been so happy, so filled with life and energy those last few months as she brought warmth and delight to our transitional home in La Cañada and to our new home in Arizona. It was like a wonderful last gift to us—to create happy memories in both places, to help us smile through our own life transition, before she slipped quietly away.

Through these losses, I learned some lessons about grieving.

I learned that grief over the loss of an animal companion is often at least as intense as the loss of a human family member or friend. This seems crazy to those who have never shared a home with or deeply loved a companion animal. For the rest of us, it can be a guilty secret as we try to go on with our lives at work and among friends and family.

But when you think about it, this intense grief makes sense.

Our animals are our daily companions. We may go weeks, months, or even years without seeing beloved (or not-so-beloved) family members.

For some, those who do not believe in an afterlife or who believe in an afterlife only for humans, the loss of a beloved pet feels jarring and final. For those who envision the Rainbow Bridge and imagine that they will be welcomed into heaven by a joyous, long-lost animal companion, some comfort exists despite the immediate sense of loss.

The love between human and companion animal is pure and unconditional. The bonds of love we have with human family members can be complicated with old hurts and resentments, current conflicts, and the complexities of the personalities involved. This is not to say the love isn't deep or real. It's simply more complicated.

We feel more responsible, in most instances, for our companion animals in a unique way. While some of us may be caregivers for parents or spouses during long, final illnesses or disabilities, and while some of us may make the difficult decision not to extend a loved one's life through extraordinary means, this decision is often made with their prior consent or as a joint decision with the loved one who is ill. With an animal companion, the decision about extending life or euthanasia is on our shoulders. While many people say that an animal will let you know when she or he is ready to leave this life, that hasn't been our experience. Freddie—in pain, bleeding heavily from his disintegrating face, and beginning to get confused as the cancer spread to his brain—continued to eat with enthusiasm, to jump six-foot fences to visit neighbors, and to patrol the neighborhood as usual on the last day of his life. What prompted the decision for euthanasia at that point was the fact that we realized that Freddie was in terrible pain.

Bob also decided to spare me the experience of seeing him die by scheduling the euthanasia while I was away on a business trip. I never second-guessed his decision. I had seen and felt Freddie wince with pain when I picked him up. I had seen him shivering and shaking in a perfectly warm room. It was time to end his suffering.

Yet that responsibility is heavy. You often wonder, "Was it too soon?" or "If he had had a voice, how would he have voted?" In some instances, it's impossible to know. All you can know is that you made the best decision you could at the time, under a trusted doctor's advice and support.

Even when there is no alternative—Timmy dying painfully from melamine poisoning, Marina's organs shutting down in end-state leukemia—the decision to end that treasured little life is incredibly difficult.

What can make the loss of a companion animal particularly difficult, too, is that you don't always get the support you would like, the support you need, from others—even from close friends and family.

When Freddie died and I found myself fighting tears at work, a coworker who was also a friend shocked me by saying, with an edge of impatience, "Kathy, I'm sorry. But remember, he was just a cat. It isn't like someone in your family died. It could be worse."

"Freddie was a member of my family," I said, a little angry and a little ashamed to admit to someone who obviously didn't and couldn't understand the depth of my feelings for this longtime pet.

My coworker gave me a sideways look that said, "Crazy cat lady!" and we spoke of it no more. But several years later, she adopted her first pet, a lively and affectionate little mixed-breed dog. One day, over lunch, she apologized to me for her insensitivity to my grief over Freddie.

"I had no idea then how much an animal could mean to you," she said. "Now I do. I really think I understand. If . . . when . . . Joey dies, it will be like losing a family member for sure. He is my dearest family member. He is the most loving. I can't even think of losing him. . . ." Her eyes filled with tears.

ENDURING LESSONS FOR THE GRIEVING PROCESS

In my own journey through the grief of losing three beloved cats, I've learned more than I ever imagined about the process. These are the lessons I'd like to share.

❖ **Grieve in your own unique ways.** Cry when you need to. Allow yourself to feel whatever comes up—whether anger or guilt or overwhelming sadness. Perhaps write poetry or journal about your animal companion and the feelings of loss you have. Find comfort, for a time, in something that was meaningful to your pet.

The daughter of a friend of ours wore her cat's collar as a wristband while she was grieving the loss of her eighteen-year-old cat. It reminded me of an incident when we had just lost Freddie. He loved his collars, especially the one he wore the last two years of his life. It was bright red with rhinestones, and he would prance around with his head held high, showing it off when we had company. Soon after his death, I saw Bob holding that collar and, though he was weeping, finding some solace in the connection to Freddie. Today, that collar still rests on top of Freddie's urn.

It may be comforting, too, to do some deep breathing and meditation to still the turmoil within. Give yourself the gift of time to replenish your spirit with deep, healing breaths and the peace that can come from living for a moment in the present—giving yourself a break from yearning for what was and dreading the time ahead without that beloved animal. Let yourself relax into the present for a moment, then another.

Don't let your grieving process be dictated by others. Who says you shouldn't cry or talk about your loss or, if it brings you comfort, hold a favorite possession of your cat's? If you don't get the support you need from those closest to you, seek it elsewhere. But don't hide or deny the feelings of grief just because someone else thinks it's silly to mourn a companion animal.

🐾 **Seek support from those who understand instead of isolating yourself.** This support may come from friends and relatives who have loved and lost an animal companion. It may come from a local pet-loss support group, which are available in many cities nationwide. It may even come online.

Two services in particular can be immensely helpful to those grieving the loss of a pet. One is a website, another a hotline.

Petloss.com is a website for pet lovers grieving the loss of a pet or experiencing anticipatory grief over a pet who is terminally ill. As well as offering a state-by-state guide to pet-loss support groups, this site offers chat rooms and supportive, ongoing online conversations about experiences with loss. (Some of the topics the last time I checked included the long-lasting impact of losing a pet and the unexpected intensity of grief, with warm and supportive comments from readers.) There is also a page for poetry and a Monday memorial/celebration-of-life ceremony online.

The ASPCA offers a Pet Loss Hotline where you can talk with someone about your grief or about making the decision for euthanasia. The hotline number is: 877-GRIEF-10.

Give yourself time to let go gradually of reminders instead of instantly obliterating all traces of your lost animal in an effort to quiet your grief. Throwing out all of your pet's toys and bedding will not still the torment within.

Give yourself time to decide what to let go of and what to keep—perhaps for another animal.

Some possessions at times need to be discarded quickly. When Marina died of leukemia, we immediately discarded her bedding and toys just as a safeguard to our surviving, uninfected cats and those to come. This step can be necessary in cases of communicable infections.

In most cases, however, you can take the time you need to decide what to discard or give away and what to keep. After finding Timmy's beloved red ribbon behind a file cabinet in my professional office, we kept it for a while and then, preparing for our move to Arizona, we decided, at last, to let it go. We realized that we had other reminders of Timmy that were more a part of our daily lives.

One of these is Timmy's basket. It is a small wicker basket with a handle that we bought for Timmy after Gus grew too large and less inclined to share a basket they had both enjoyed since kittenhood. We thought that this basket was too small for Gus and just right for Timmy. It was an instant hit with Timmy—and also with Gus, who found a way to squeeze himself into it when Timmy wasn't looking. Although we still call it Timmy's basket, it has been a favorite of all the cats who have come after—and that makes our hearts glad.

✿ Realize that the grief process isn't a straight and orderly path. Most of us are familiar with the stages of grief identified by Elisabeth Kübler-Ross: denial and isolation, anger, bargaining, depression, acceptance.

All of those can happen in the wake of a pet's death, but it isn't an orderly process.

There may be days when you think you've reached some level of acceptance, only to find yourself the next day struggling once again with depression and anger. It can be a matter of taking two steps forward and one back, or one forward and two back. The progress through grief is very individual, very uneven.

Allow yourself those setbacks. They're going to happen. Just as you're feeling that life is going on, there is a reminder, a memory of the animal you've lost, that takes you back into the most painful parts of your grief. Then you feel better again. And so it goes, through the weeks and months and years.

As the adage goes, time heals, but this is only partly true. With time, the sharpness and immediacy of loss are tempered by healing and growth and new experiences. But the loss is always there. Sometimes you feel it with particular poignancy, even years after the loss.

And sometimes you experience your loss in a more positive way, with warm gratitude for having known and loved this special animal, as well as sadness that this beloved animal is no longer with you.

❖ **Find comfort and healing in warm memories.** Initially, when we lose a beloved animal companion, the magnitude of the loss overshadows everything. But as the days go by without your treasured friend, there can be comfort and healing in remembering all that was wonderful, all that you loved. These memories can bring tears. But they can also bring moments of joy. The opportunities to remember are all around you.

I remember Marina with a smile whenever I polish our granite kitchen counters. She only lived in our Arizona home for the last three weeks of her life, but she made it her own—and rolling around on the granite countertops (when she thought I wasn't looking) was one of her greatest pleasures. Although I generally have a low tolerance for cats on countertops, I couldn't help but smile at Marina's pleasure and exuberance then and now when I remember.

While I remember with great pleasure many stories and moments with Timmy and Marina—and our first cat

Freddie, too—there are sense memories, remembered moments of a feeling, a sensation, that comfort as well. I remember the soft feel and scent of Marina's fur and the delight of her musical trills, the peace and understanding in Timmy's eyes. These can help bring about a sense of calm—and visibly lower my blood pressure during a test— as much as imagining the gentle surf in Maui.

As much as we mourn our pets who have passed away, there are so many reasons to rejoice in the fact that we knew them, embracing them and giving them good lives. Even the most satisfying and inspiring love stories of our lives—animal and human—end in loss. The memories that remain can remind us of the blessing of having loved.

❖ **Allow joy between your moments of pain.** For most of us, feelings of grief come in waves, with moments of calm in between, as we go about our lives as necessary— working, caring for others, or tackling household tasks. To find joy between the moments of pain, we may allow ourselves to be pleased about a job well done, warmed by a smile or kind word from another, comforted by a sweet memory, or enjoy a moment of humor and healing laughter.

Some feel guilty and push joy away as they grieve for a lost loved one, convinced that finding joy in the midst of pain minimizes the loss. But joy can be a vital part of healing. When you allow yourself to feel joy between those waves of pain, it can give you strength for the next pain, the strength to live through your loss. Far from dismissing your grief and loss as inconsequential, embracing joy during those lovely, lengthening times between your bouts of grieving can integrate this loss into your life and make it possible to take the risk of loving again.

❖ Open your heart to other animals. Some people are so grief-stricken after the loss of a beloved pet that they can't imagine ever having another animal and they vow never to go this way again.

My friend Chuck was so distraught after his beloved dachshund Zachary died at age eighteen that he swore he would never have another pet. "I can't put myself through this horror of loss again," he told me. "It's too much. I just can't do it."

Others rush to get another pet to "replace" the one who was lost—and find themselves disappointed with the differences they see between the cherished animal who was lost and the newcomer to the household.

In both cases, people may make mistakes.

While it's painfully true that we usually outlive our treasured animals, the love and joy they bring to our lives make the risk of loss and grief well worth taking. While people can have good reasons for not getting another pet—being in the middle of a life transition, a change of lifestyle that includes more travel, marriage to a partner who has allergies or who dislikes animals—it's a choice worth considering.

On the other hand, rushing to get a new pet while still actively grieving the lost one can lead to disappointment and possible unnecessary rejection of the new animal.

My friend Monica lost a dog who was, truly, among the world's finest a year ago. Her dog was beautiful, wonderfully behaved, friendly, and immensely loving. Although she waited six months before adopting another animal, her grief was still too profound to allow her to bond with this new pet. The little poodle she brought home was sweet, but a little rambunctious, a little anxious. In her grief, she didn't make allowances, not only for the fact that each animal is unique, but also for the fact that all animals need a period of adjustment to a new home. She returned the little dog to the rescue organization after less than a day and is continuing to grieve.

Pet-loss literature often suggests that a person wait at least a month after the death of a pet before considering adopting a new one. Obviously, readiness to open one's heart to another varies widely from person to person. Some may be ready for a new companion animal in a month. Some may need many months, a year, or longer before they feel free to love another animal.

Trust your own sense of what is right for you when deciding whether or when to open your heart and your home to a new companion animal.

🐾 **Realize that no animal can replace another.** Each animal is unique. You will never find a cat or dog like the one you lost. Even if you choose the same breed, even if the old pet and new pet resemble each other, you won't find a true replacement. Interestingly, this is true even with cloned animals—an expensive exercise in attempted pet replacement. In the few instances where a cat has been cloned, the new kitten may not even look like the original and may have a completely different personality. Who our pets are, after all, is not only genetic, but also a matter of their personal histories and experiences.

Since losing Timmy and Marina, we have opened our hearts and home to three new animals—all completely unlike our beloved therapy cats despite some similarities in breed.

Maggie, whom I introduced in chapter 6, is a black Bombay—a mixture of sable Burmese and black American shorthair—who was dumped into rescue by a Beverly Hills breeder because she was such an ugly kitten. We adopted her as a kitten in 2007 about a month after Timmy's death to soothe Gus, who was howling in the night for his lost brother. Gus and Maggie have bonded wonderfully and she has captured our hearts as well. Bob is her primary person, and she grooms him and Gus on a daily basis. She looks nothing like Timmy, has her own unique personality, is shy with strangers, and shares only a few aspects of their partial Burmese heritage: the skinny tail, the intelligence, the occasional obsession, the tiny but heavy feet. We have learned to value her for the wonderful cat that she is and don't expect her to be anything but herself.

Marina's death in May 2010 was especially difficult—in part, because she was so wonderful and in part because she died at a time when we had just finished a major relocation and were far from old friends and all that was familiar in our lives. I found myself longing for another cat like Marina who loved to be held for hours, who thrived on attention, who had Siamese intelligence and tabby warmth. In my longings, I violated one of the lessons I should have known—that no cat ever replaces another.

About a month after losing Marina, I searched online for another flame-point Siamese, alerting rescue groups that I was ready and willing to adopt one immediately. There were no flame-point Siamese kittens or cats in rescue at that time, but one organization in Casa Grande—about forty miles from our new home—had a lynx point/ Siamese-mix kitten. I saw the picture of a little white cat with blue eyes and faint black and gray markings online and decided she was perfect, without having met her. Her shelter name was Sweet Pea.

I contacted the animal shelter. Sweet Pea hadn't done well there, I was told. She was in a foster home being nurtured and hand fed until she weighed two pounds and was ready for adoption. She had been found, four weeks old and all alone, wandering by the entrance of the shelter—which was in an isolated area in the middle of the desert. No one had any idea how she got there.

Shelter staff put me in email contact with her "foster mom," Colleen, who told me that Sweet Pea was lively, funny, feisty, and thriving. She told me that this one had a larger-than-life personality. "My husband and I call her the Pea Who Will Take Over the World," she laughed.

I think I heard what I wanted to hear: funny and thriving. Had I been listening, "larger than life" and "feisty" would have been better clues to the cat I was proposing to adopt.

On the day set for our adoption, Colleen and her husband, Dave, brought Sweet Pea to the shelter in one of their own cat carriers. Swiftly and without ceremony, they transferred her to our carrier, we signed on the dotted line, and they vanished. We headed for home with our new kitten.

It wasn't long before we were asking ourselves, *What were we thinking?*

Sweet Pea was—and is—not only the complete opposite of Marina, but also totally unlike any cat we've ever had. Despite her tiny size, she was incredibly fierce. When Gus came to welcome her with a soft nuzzle, she bit him in the face. She hissed and growled at Maggie for weeks. And once past her moments of vulnerability as a small kitten, she wouldn't let us touch her or pick her up. She has wonderfully soft fur and a beautiful face, but the greatest impression she made on us, at least initially, was the sharpness of her teeth and claws.

Although we had times when we were tempted to return her to the shelter, we have always believed that, when you adopt, you make a commitment to the animal for life. We were also convinced that long-term, consistent love would win her over.

In the meantime, we amused ourselves with a series of descriptive nicknames like "Wild Weasel" and "Rabid Badger," which pretty much summed up her behavior and temperament. She was the anti-Marina, the feline equivalent of the Antichrist.

Gus and Maggie learned to give her a lot of space and stopped trying to include her in mutual grooming.

Only once did she inspire a feline intervention on her behalf. One evening, while still a half-grown kitten, she had attacked Gus, biting him hard in the face and stomach, one time too many. This usually affable large male cat suddenly lost it and flattened her against the tile floor. She screamed in terror. From another room, Maggie came running. Maggie smacked Gus on the head, and he released the yowling kitten. Then Maggie stood between Gus and Sweet Pea and stared at him intently. He shambled away, and Maggie started grooming the shaken kitten.

This wasn't the start of new warmth between Maggie and Sweet Pea, but it was the end of Sweet Pea's bold attacks on the larger cats.

Bob and I dedicated ourselves to immersing Sweet Pea in love. We talked softly to her, telling her how happy we were that she had joined our family. We touched her whenever she would allow it. We gave her special treats.

With time, she calmed down and became less hostile. She began to crave proximity to her people—following us from room to room, wanting to be wherever we were, sitting by me at the computer with her head resting on one of my hands as I typed. As more time passed, she became a little friendlier with the other cats and sought petting from us at times of her choice. She started cuddling beside me as I sat on the couch reading newspapers. She now spends hours in Bob's lap and is starting to beg for attention from both of us.

Some aspects of the Rabid Badger persist, however. Unasked-for petting can lead to a light bite. Picking her up is still right up there on our list of risk-taking behaviors, living on the edge.

But, four years later, Sweet Pea is a much more loving and affection-ate animal. She even welcomes visitors to the house with tiny trills and leg rubs. A large part of Sweet Pea's progress has been our love despite her hair-trigger temper, our acceptance of her as is: we touch her only when she asks us to. She runs a tight ship with firm boundaries, and we've learned to respect those. When she feels safe—and respected— she can be quite wonderful.

On a June day in 2012, two years into our efforts to socialize Sweet Pea, there was an email from another rescue organization, about forty

miles in yet another direction: they had—at last—a flame-point Siamese kitten, a two-month-old male, available for adoption.

We both hesitated. We had our hands full with Sweet Pea. And
yet . . .

"Maybe a little kitten would be good for her, someone to play
with," Bob said.

"Another flame-point is very tempting," I said.

Bob laughed. "But this time, we won't make any commitment
beforehand. We'll go spend time with this kitten and see what he's
like before we agree to adopt him."

He was wonderful. A sweet, beautiful little kitten whose shelter
name was "Prince Charming," he cuddled and purred immediately.
The woman who had fostered him as a newborn wept as we signed
the papers to adopt him. "I just love him so much," she said, wiping her tears with the back of her hand. "He's just a wonderful little
kitten."

His beginnings, they told us, had been less than optimal: his
mother was a throwaway, once a pet, now abandoned, and she gave
birth to this little white kitten in the yard of a residence not far from
the animal shelter. From that day on, Prince Charming was dearly
loved in a foster home where he was nurtured, socialized, and adored
before being made available for adoption.

We decided, after our Sweet Pea experience, to change his so-sweet
shelter name immediately, noting that our testy Sweet Pea and the
memory of my beloved Aunt Molly's nightmare of a surly cat named
Sugar were powerful arguments against sweet names.

We decided to call him Hamish, nickname "Hammie."

Hammie was an instant hit with Gus and Maggie. Gus embraced him warmly and immediately. Maggie groomed him constantly and made sure he got his fair share of food. Sweet Pea was not amused. She smacked him in the face with a paw. He smacked her back. She ran to us whimpering with surprise.

Although a flame-point Siamese like Marina, Hammie bears little resemblance to our late therapy cat. Except for his ears, tail, and blue eyes, his face and body markings are quite different from Marina's. He has the broad, jowly face of a large male cat with none of Marina's delicacy. And he has a legacy from his Siamese heritage that Marina never shared: he is cross-eyed. It adds considerably to his charm.

Hammie is, without a doubt, a charmer. He embraces and grooms Gus, frail in his sixteenth year. He cuddles with Maggie. He wrestles and plays with Sweet Pea, sometimes a bit more vigorously than she would like, and then they groom each other. He has a wonderful routine of affection with Bob and me—greeting me with purrs and rubs every time I emerge from the shower; cuddling beside Bob as he meditates or does sit-ups; curling up by our heads, purring, when we're reading; talking to us in a wonderful mixture of chirps and trills that remind us of two vocal, much loved cats. But we love and accept Hammie as a unique creature.

Our love for Gus, now sixteen, is very special. He is a living link between the past and the present, the only cat we've had who has known every other cat. He was a loving kitten with an aged and dying Freddie, cuddling up to warm him as he lay shivering and near death. He was a loving and devoted brother to Timmy. He happily welcomed

Marina to our home, and, though she was cool to him much of the time, he was by her side in an instant when he heard her in distress as she neared death. He has nurtured Maggie and Hammie as kittens as well as doing his best to extend such nurturing to Sweet Pea, who now has a reasonably warm relationship with him. And he has been a very special love in our lives.

Gus, above all, has been there for Bob at times of depression and during night terrors, throwing himself on Bob's chest, embracing him and purring, or lying across his legs in an effort to calm him. Gus has been my most constant feline companion over the years, always eager to cuddle, quick to purr.

As Gus grows frail and struggles to walk, as his eyesight fades, we sometimes have a stab of anticipatory grief, knowing that our time together is approaching the end—that, sooner rather than later, we will experience another painful and totally unique loss, the loss of a dearly loved cat who, more than any other, is a natural therapy cat with us. He is always there for us with a purr and a loving touch. He is there with us in distress and in celebration. He is uniquely peaceful and delightful to be with. He still finds joy in loving and being loved. We treasure each day shared with him.

There will never be another Gus. Or Timmy and Marina. Or Maggie or Hammie. Or, quite certainly, another Sweet Pea. Each relationship we have with our companion animals is a blessing.

We will always grieve those beloved animals lost. The key is to treasure their memories while making room in our hearts for another new, totally unique little life.

Fourteen:

THE LEGACY OF TIMMY AND MARINA

Timmy and Marina live on in our hearts and warm memories. The cats we found by chance, the cats who accidentally showed their talents as therapy cats, were simply meant to be, to bless our lives, first and foremost, as beloved animal companions.

They have a dual legacy: what they leave behind for those who knew them as simply wonderful cats and what stays with those who experienced them as therapy cats.

The legacy they leave for Bob and me, for family and friends who also knew them and cared, is one of love: experiences, memories, and lessons in love.

Some of these personal lessons endure, warming our lives and relationships.

Timmy and Marina taught me the value of cultivating love instead of simply expecting it. There are cats—and there are people—who simply feel deserving of love and are delighted to be on the receiving end of another's tender feelings. Others realize that building a lasting, resilient love takes care and effort and giving at least as much as receiving.

Timmy and Marina were not cats who simply happily accepted attention, petting, and soft endearments. They were active participants in building bonds with the humans in their lives. Perhaps it was the result of having been throwaways. Timmy and his siblings were tossed into a dump and left to die as three-week-old kittens, far too young to survive on their own. Marina was adopted and abandoned by two families, the last because they found her too emotionally needy. These two wonderful cats never took love and attention for granted. They actively sought love by giving it in so many different ways: Timmy with his exuberant greetings and hours of cuddling Bob, kissing him as he curled around his shoulders, carrying on lively conversations with him; Marina with her trilled songs, kisses, and cuddling with me on my pillow at night. They were a presence—actively loving family members.

We found that this cultivation of love worked in the other direction, too. It worked on taming our wild Sweet Pea. It also helped Gus at a pivotal point in his life.

When Timmy and his brother Gus were not quite a year old, we noticed that Gus, a quieter, less outgoing cat, was withdrawing even further. We wondered if he felt left out, unloved. It was so easy to notice and share love with Timmy, who showed his feelings so openly. But, at that point in his life, Gus was easy to overlook. Bob and I both decided to make an effort to cultivate love with this sweet cat as well. We showered him with attention and loving words, petting him at every opportunity. A very special love began to grow. As he felt our love, Gus grew in his own capacity to love and take his own special place in the family. He became a very different—and wonderful—feline companion when we stopped expecting him to be as demonstrative as Timmy and started loving him as he was— and letting him know whenever we could just how cherished he was—and is.

Timmy and Marina taught me by example to pay special attention to loved ones. Over time our lives get automated by routines, by long-held beliefs and by the delusion that we know all there is to know about those we love the most. Sometimes, as a result, we only half-listen to a loved one's words, we're too distracted by life happening around us to really look into the eyes of a partner, and we make assumptions about their feelings.

It took our therapy cats, Timmy and Marina—as well as Gus and Freddie—to teach me a different way.

I had long admired how Timmy and Marina paid attention in the therapy room, seeming to know immediately how to approach a particular client, who would welcome lap-sitting and who would prefer to play or to pet a cat from a distance. They seemed incredibly sensitive to body language and nuance, to tones of voice.

It was humbling, though, to discover that our loving cats often were more attuned to Bob's moods, more aware of what was going on with him, than I was.

Sometimes the first sign I had that Bob was slipping into another depression or that he had suffered nightmares and night terrors again was Gus, spread over Bob's chest, purring loudly to soothe him. Or it might be Timmy wrapping himself around Bob's neck and staying there, his face pressed to Bob's for hours. Or, in earlier times, it was Freddie, in Bob's lap with his front paws stretched out to embrace him, that signaled that Bob needed help and reassurance.

These loving cats taught me to pay closer attention, to be ready and willing to drop whatever it was that seemed so essential, to be there for Bob or for someone else I loved who needed extra care.

But I'm still learning—and our current therapeutic companion cats are still teaching me important lessons in paying attention, prioritizing, and compassion.

Timmy and Marina taught me to live life fully every day—all the days of my life. We humans have a number of ways we approach our lives and our mortality. Some live as if they would never die and don't want to consider their mortality. Some can think of little else.

My father was one of the latter. Part of it may have been due to his extreme Irishness—unopposed by any other ethnicities in his genetic heritage—but his twin obsessions were drink and death—and the more he drank, the more he thought of death. He was busy dying every day of his life.

Growing up, we became almost, but not quite, accustomed to his famous "death speeches," most often given when he was in bed with the flu or during the month of March (he would take to his bed every March, convinced that, like his mother, he would die during that month) or when one of us was departing for a time. "I probably will die before Christmas," he told me with tears in his eyes, just before I boarded a plane to fly to Chicago to start college. "So this is good-bye. Good-bye, my baby. You've been a wonderful daughter. I love you so much. Please remember me. . . ."

He actually died seventeen years later, on a July afternoon, while storming around his front yard yelling after an errant UPS delivery driver who, intimidated by my father's presence, had once again kicked a package off the truck at the end of the driveway and kept moving. Father's true last words are best left unprinted.

Cats are quite different in their approach to life, illness, and death. They may lack an intellectual understanding of their mortality, especially if they've been pampered house cats with no immediate experience of the death of peers. But they have an instinct, born of their wild genes, to hide any signs of illness—and to hide when incapacitated by illness so as not to be targets for predators. Humans may see this instinct as innate stoicism. What it means is that it can be very hard to diagnose illness in a cat or even if you know a cat is terminally ill, to see the end coming. Our late therapy cats and our first cat Freddie all lived their lives fully to the end.

Freddie, ill with a skin cancer that had taken much of his nose and upper lip, still ate with gusto and continued to jump tall fences to visit neighborhood friends every day of his life, including his last.

Between bouts of pain and nausea during his last two days of life at home, Timmy was eager to do what he usually did—cuddle and play and stay close to us. And Marina lived her life at our new home in Arizona with such energy and joy that we had no idea that she had reached the end stage of leukemia until her very last few days when she finally felt ill enough to withdraw and to hide under the bed.

What their end-of-life examples can teach us is the importance of savoring and living fully in each moment of our lives, not letting the prospect of death—whether distant, imminent, or unknowable—overshadow the joys and wonders of today.

Timmy and Marina helped me, in so many ways, to remember that love is all. As life speeds up and grows complicated, and as electronics too often substitute for real contact and intimacy between people, it's easy to lose sight of what is most important, what will always be most essential in our lives: love.

For some people—busy with careers and achievements and upward mobility or engaged in a struggle simply to get a foothold in a middle-class life—love is something to be deferred.

A longtime friend of mine who is an actor nearing the end of his life now regrets the many times he gave career advancement first priority.

"Love was an inconvenience," he says. "It was something that could wait until I had reached a certain level of success as an actor. But I'd reach one level and decide that I wasn't quite there yet and so I spent all those years chasing success when friends and family knew what I should have known all along: that loving and being loved matters most in life and that, with a loving partner beside you, so much more is possible. I was so focused on getting this role or that one, on being seen and noticed, that I let love slip away from me too many times. I feel very blessed, as a foolish old man, that I have some nieces, my late sister's daughters, who bring so much love and caring to my life."

It's a lesson we learn from family and friends and even from strangers who reach the end of their lives only to find that all those things they thought were essential to a happy, fulfilling life were, in fact, not the answer to their yearnings for meaning, particularly as time was running out.

For Bob and me, the death of family and friends, as much as these events affected us emotionally, were not immediate experiences. Every member of the older generations in my family—parents, aunts, grandmother—died suddenly of heart attacks and, in one instance, of a massive stroke, often without previous signs of illness. Their deaths were news—devastating news in some instances—rather than shared experiences. In Bob's family, his grandparents and parents lived and passed away at distances too great for him to reach in time to share their last moments.

We learned about the power of love with new intensity and immediacy from Timmy and Marina.

In their last moments of life—after all the medical interventions; the irrational, tortured hopes for recovery; the frantic search for help and answers—what remained was, simply and extraordinarily, love.

In Timmy's last seconds of life, as he heard the love in Bob's voice, his terror abated and his connection to Bob was all as he looked into his eyes and eased into his arms. His eyes were filled with love and peace as Bob's arms enveloped him. Nothing else mattered—as he left his life knowing that he was dearly loved.

Marina, too, knew only love in her last seconds of life. When I touched her as she lay on the table, awaiting that last injection as her body systems were failing, her eyes met mine with a powerful and all-encompassing love. Her last gift was to put her head in my hand and continue to look at us with incredible tenderness as she passed so quietly from this life.

Their deaths—as sad, as devastating as they were—were also indelible lessons in the power and primacy of love in our lives.

We will never forget these lessons or these very special cats—or ever stop feeling blessed that these wonderful animals came into our lives.

But what about their lasting legacy with the patients whose lives they touched? We may never know.

The impact of therapy cats can be subtle, much like the impact of therapists, on the lives of the people who come to talk, to cry, and to share feelings for a session or two, or for months or for years. Whatever the length of their treatment, there is always a parting. And often you never know how much—or if—you were able to help them.

So many factors drive people's anxieties, depressions, compulsions, and the other conditions that complicate their lives. These can't necessarily be fixed or completely resolved in the number of sessions permitted by an insurance company or even after years of self-paid therapy. You hope to make a difference—to provide some peace, some respite, some tools for them to use in continuing to work on these and other conflicts in the future.

But much of the time, you never know. Many patients leave and you never hear from them again. I would always leave it to the patient to stay in touch—or not. Most prefer to move on with their lives and not to look back. For many, that is a healthy, desirable outcome. For others, maintaining a warm connection is equally healthy. It all depends on the individual and the issues he or she brought to therapy.

The minority of patients who have stayed in touch, are, for the most part, patients with whom I worked over a long period of time. Even then, the feedback is as varied as the people involved.

Sometimes the feedback is a brief but heartfelt email, like Julia's sweet remembrance of Timmy as unforgettable in the wake of his death.

Even more rarely comes a continuing warm relationship that evolves into a friendship. My former patient Mariana was one of those, and a major fan of Timmy's for the rest of her life. After her heart finally failed and she died in her sleep in 2008, the friendship has continued with her daughter Diana, who not only remembers how much her mother enjoyed both the idea and the reality of Timmy (and his brother Gus) but also what it meant for her to connect with me in therapy and, later on, as a friend. "It was so good for her to have someone else to talk with besides me," she told me recently. "That's why I urged her to come back that second time and try to find a way to connect with you. I felt the possibility was there. And she was so excited to find that you were an animal lover, too. That was the beginning of everything."

Some clients are very clear about what therapy has meant to them, yet they may still surprise you with a takeaway life change.

Chloe, who was, at ten years, my client with the longest tenure, keeps in touch via email and occasional phone calls since my move to Arizona. She has told me fervently and often that our work together was pivotal to her life, that I may well have saved her life. And she always seems a bit surprised when I emphasize the courage and openness to growth on her part that made such a positive outcome possible.

Our parting, as therapist and patient, happened when I moved to Arizona, and it was not easy initially. At first, she requested telephone therapy sessions on an emergency basis. I encouraged her to continue with another therapist for in-person sessions, and she has done so. She has also integrated the many healthy aspects of her life to maintain the momentum of her emotional growth—the support of her wonderful, insightful husband; her delight in watching her son, now approaching adolescence, excel in school and grow into a caring young man; and close relationships with some very special friends. And yet she can surprise me—as she did recently.

Chloe was my one Saturday client who was allergic to cats, and so she was always my first patient of the day and never laid eyes on Timmy or Marina—although she was the only patient I saw who was with me throughout the years that I offered the services of both therapy cats. She loved the idea of animal-assisted therapy, and she often wished she could meet and spend time with those cats on the other side of the office bathroom door. Now, she recently told me, she is in training with her dog to offer animal-assisted services through a volunteer organization at area hospitals, schools, and nursing homes.

On the other end of the feedback spectrum, I recently got a call from Joe Jr. wanting to do a telephone session due to issues with his girlfriend.

As I was searching my calendar for possible appointment times, he asked politely what I was up to these days. I told him that I was writing a book about my therapy cats.

"Therapy cats?" he laughed. "You had therapy cats?"

I stopped looking through the calendar, momentarily stunned. "Yes," I said. "As a matter of fact, you and your dad worked with one of them—Marina. Don't you remember?"

There was a pause, then laughter on the other end of the line. "Oh, yeah," he said at last. "You mean that little white cat that used to shed all over my dad!"

So therapy cats' legacies can run the full spectrum with clients— from animals who helped to facilitate life-changing therapy to mere shedders. But I know, because I was there, that what Timmy and Marina did with and for clients did matter at the time—whether it was Timmy helping Julia to feel more loveable, Irene to release her burden of bitterness, or Peter to rediscover the value of play—or whether it was Marina helping the two Joes to improve their communication by speaking to each other in more civilized tones.

The efforts of Timmy and Marina blended with my efforts with clients during a time when our lives all converged. Now they and I—perhaps having played a part in making a difference in the life of another, perhaps not—are faint memories for most. And that is the order of things as time goes on.

As my new life in Arizona has evolved, Bob and I are still greatly enjoying the company of our four cats—Gus, Maggie, Sweet Pea, and Hammie. Each, in his or her own way, is a wonderful companion animal.

But I may have another potential therapy cat in the making. He brings back so many memories from the past.

Hammie is a flame-point Siamese like Marina with a temperament faintly reminiscent of Timmy's—though he is wonderfully and uniquely himself. He cuddles Gus, frail at sixteen, with great tenderness. And he can't stay away from someone in distress. He is quick to cuddle with Bob in down moments, and, as I recently sighed and put my head in my hands, momentarily stressed by a work deadline, I felt a soft paw stroking my back. It was Hammie. I couldn't help smiling.

But Hammie isn't just therapeutic to the family. He recently demonstrated his potential as a therapy cat when he extended his comfort to a stranger.

Our neighbor Phyllis is a gracious hostess who usually prefers that we socialize at her home, three doors down. She and her husband, Wally, are dear friends of ours, but Phyllis is a relative stranger to our cats. One day not long ago, however, she was feeling particularly distressed and came over to our house to talk.

Phyllis' declining health has been a major concern lately. She has advanced cancer and is getting chemotherapy. She is also suffering from kidney failure, necessitating dialysis treatments three times a week. A recent setback, complications in her dialysis, had reduced her to tears as she sat on our couch talking about her fears.

Suddenly, I was aware of Hammie, coming out of nowhere, jumping up on the couch beside her. Watching closely, I held my breath.

Phyllis is a dog person who doesn't much like cats. I hoped his presence wouldn't upset her further.

Hammie stretched out on the couch, placing his front paws softly on her leg, looking up at her, watching, not moving.

Finally, in midsentence, she stopped and looked down at him. They simply sat there together, communing quietly for a few minutes.

And then, her tears momentarily forgotten, Phyllis smiled. Hammie rested his head on his paws and purred, still looking at her with sweet compassion.

And so love and hope live on.

Sweet Pea

Gus and Hamish

Marina

ACKNOWLEDGMENTS

My special thanks to:

My agent Gene Brissie of James Peter Associates, who has been encouraging me to write from the heart for the past thirty-five years—first as an editor, then as a publisher, and now as my agent. I am so grateful for his wisdom, support, and friendship over the years.

Allison Janse, my editor at HCI, for saying "Yes!" to this story I've been wanting to tell for so long about my therapy cats and for her warm encouragement and excellent suggestions throughout my work on this book.

My former agent Susan Ann Protter, who is now happily retired, for her enthusiasm for this idea and for the pleasure of her continuing friendship after nearly forty years of working together.

Three very special veterinarians who appear in this book and who have been important in the lives of our cherished cats: Dr.

Tracy McFarland, who rescued Timmy and Gus and from whom we adopted them, and who cared for our cats Freddie, Timmy, Gus, Maggie, and Marina over the years; Dr. Sean Yoshimoto of VCA West Los Angeles, who treated Timmy in his last hours and who comforted him—and us—at his death; and Dr. Wendy Holst, now of Paws Veterinary Clinic in Mesa, Arizona, who showed extraordinary kindness and support during Marina's illness and death and who has given wonderful care to our cats Gus, Maggie, Sweet Pea, and Hamish since our move to Arizona.

To friends who gave special encouragement and support during my work on this book, including Tim Schellhardt (who urged me on with daily email nudges), Mary and John Breiner, Ryan Grady, Pat Hill, Kim Tuomi, Phyllis and Walter Skurda, Kelly Hartwig, Marsha Morello, Joe Shea, Stella Natelli, Chuck Wibbelsman, Michael Polich, Maurice Sherbanee, Sr. Rita McCormack, Sr. Ramona Bascom, Jeanne and Jimmy Yagi, Mary Kate Schellhardt and Matt Palko, Eliza and Chris Yarbrough, Jeanie Croope, Dee Ready, Shelly Morales, Peggy Vork-Zambory, Rosaria Williams, Barbara Ferrell, Maggie Mallard, Sally Wessely, Janet Pegram, Mary Vaughn, Jennifer Rourke, Dorothy and Darrian Dusa, Daniel Wetmore, and Cindy and Tom Miller, and to my family: Tai and Nick McCoy, Mike, Jinjuta, Maggie and Henry McCoy, and Caron and Bud Roudebush.

Finally, heartfelt thanks to my husband, Bob Stover, who helped immensely with this book by sharing his own memories of and insights about Timmy and Marina, expert proofreading, and much appreciated encouragement all along the way.

ABOUT THE AUTHOR

Kathy McCoy, PhD, has spent her writing career chronicling the joy, the pain, and the possibilities of life changes from adolescence to older age in more than a dozen books, including *The Teenage Body Book*, winner of the American Library Association Award for Best Book for Young Adults; in hundreds of articles for national magazines; and now in her popular blog "Living Fully in Midlife and Beyond," which averages nearly 20,000 page views a month.

Dr. McCoy is also a licensed marriage and family therapist with years of experience in working with adults, adolescents, couples, families, and those with life-changing illnesses or injuries.

Her articles have appeared in *Readers Digest, Redbook, Glamour, Ladies Home Journal, Family Circle, Woman's Day,* the *New York Times,* and the *Journal of Clinical Child Psychology.* She is a former editor of *TEEN* magazine and a former columnist for *Seventeen.* She has been a frequent guest on national television shows, including two appearances on *Oprah* and many on the *Today* show.

Dr. McCoy and her husband, Bob Stover, recently moved from Los Angeles to rural Arizona where they live with their four cats, Gus, Maggie, Sweet Pea, and Hamish.

Dr. McCoy's website is *www.drkathymccoy.com.*

Other Books by Kathy McCoy, PhD

Aging and Other Surprises

Making Peace With Your Adult Children

The Teenage Body Book (with Charles Wibbelsman, MD)

Understanding Your Teenager's Depression:
Issues, Insights, and Practical Guidance for Parents

The Secrets of My Life

Growing and Changing: A Guide for Preteens
(with Charles Wibbelsman, MD)

Life Happens (with Charles Wibbelsman, MD)

Crisis-Proof Your Teenager (with Charles Wibbelsman, MD)

Changes and Choices: A Junior High Survival Guide

Solo Parenting: Your Essential Guide

Coping with Teenage Depression

The Teenage Body Book Guide to Sexuality

The Teenage Body Book Guide to Dating

The Teenage Survival Guide